China at the Beginning of the 21st Century

Series editor: Joanna Wardęga

China at the Beginning of the 21st Century

Edited by Łukasz Gacek and Ewa Trojnar

Jagiellonian University Press

Series: Chińskie Drogi

This publication was supported by the Jagiellonian University Centre for Chinese Language and Culture "Confucius Institute in Krakow"

Reviewer
Professor Hubert Królikowski, PhD

Cover design
Ewa Skrzypiec
Photo on the cover: Joanna Wardęga

ISBN 978-83-233-3590-0

www.wuj.pl

Jagiellonian University Press
Office: ul. Michałowskiego 9/2, 31-126 Kraków
Phone: 12-631-18-81, 12-631-18-82, Fax: 12-631-18-83
Distribution: Phone: 12-631-01-97, Fax: 12-631-01-98
Cell Phone: +48-506-006-674, e-mail: sprzedaz@wuj.pl
Bank: PEKAO SA, IBAN PL 80 1240 4722 1111 0000 4856 3325

Contents

Acknowledgements

Our special thanks go to all the authors of this book for their patience and diligence, as it took time to finalize the project. We hope this experience was constructive, as your professional careers have just recently started.

Both the conference, held in 2010, and the publishing process would have not been concluded without the support from the Confucius Institute in Kraków.

Preface

China at the beginning of the 21st century intrigues many researchers around the world. No different was the enthusiasm widely shared among the participants of the students' conference *China at the Beginning of the 21st Century* organized by the Institute of Middle and Far East Studies of Jagiellonian University in Kraków in April 2010. Two days of sessions gathered many observers; moreover, a lively and collaborative working environment was created. Research enthusiasm and inquisitive attitude of presenters and discussants observed during the conference inspired us to go beyond the university walls and put this publication together.

The problems discussed within this volume provide the readers with a background of most vital issues in modern China. They are related to the challenges of the Chinese society and state's international skirmishes. While the first articles provide the insight into social change, creating tremendous opportunities, and no less significant threats for the country's future development, the others look further and beyond borders to focus our attention on security issues. Each article is separately concluded by the author's findings, which is highly admirable, since the authors are young, but promising adepts in the field. At the same time, being open for criticism, the authors invite us to take a long hard look at China's modern challenges.

The book opens with a chapter written by Natalia Ożegalska-Łukasik. While referring to rapid economic development of China and reforms initiated by Deng Xiaoping she presents a problem of internal migration on the example of the *dagongmei,* a well-known Chinese term in international academia and media describing young female workers in China. The author not only tries to convince the readers of the significance of this phenomenon, but also of its contribution to China's modernization.

An even more vibrant impact of the social change could be observed online, proves Agnieszka Szajna-Węgrzyn in Chapter Two. She touches the issue of unique Internet communication in Chinese and analyses its forms and features. Her findings indicate that the Chinese society is deeply influenced by a variety of factors among which the predominance of English usage is only lesser to the Mandarin and Chinese dialects. Noticeably, communication is rooted in sociocultural context, but portrays the users as firmly linked to the world wide web.

In Chapter Three, Michał Witek, assess position and role of Chinese contemporary art. In order to unravel its intricacy, he provides the readers with a good review of its origins. He points out Chinese economic development as a milestone of art market, which has also been profoundly analyzed.

In Chapter Fourth Janusz Bąbel presented the reforms of the Chinese military structures from 1978 when Deng Xiaoping's 'open policy' was initiated. The author analyzed these problems relating them to the changing military doctrine. In his opinion the modernization of the army with the use of advanced technologies could create new purposes in Chinese foreign policy, and could take new initiatives not only in the close neighborhood of the Middle Kingdoms.

A similar topic was also taken up in the next chapter. Its author, Paweł Bieńkowski, underlined that nowadays a gradual decrease of the role of the People's Liberation Army Chinese after the Maoist period can be observed. He also presented a very interesting issue of military and national-party connections.

In Chapter Six, Tobiasz Targosz described the issue of China's involvement in neighboring Myanmar. The author notices the practical dimension of this cooperation, pointing at the concentration of Chinese interests in the economical issues. Myanmar is a strategic partner of China, especially in the energy field. In Beijing's plans Myanmar is also treated as a bridge linking China with other countries of Southern Asia and South-East Asia.

The topic of China's energy security was also taken up by Anna Kotfis in Chapter Seven. The analysis was concentrated on Russia and Central-Asian countries. Low reserves of crude oil and natural gas force China to seek new markets abroad. Russia, with its large-scale resources, becomes a desired partner. Chinese activity in Central Asia is being determined through geopolitical elements, as well as the possibility of satisfying energy needs.

The next chapters by Karol Bronicki and Jacek Budziaszek concentrate on the Chinese territorial disputes. The first refers to Chinese-Japanese conflict in the East China Sea. The second describes the unsolved disputes in the South China Sea. In both chapters the authors emphasized the strategic dimension of rivalry. The importance of these territories was highlighted in the economic, transport, as well as fishery meaning. They also underlined their potential in the energy field, because of its oil and gas reserves.

In the last chapter Paulina Opacka described the event connected with the takeover of Hong Kong by China in 1997 and its results. The author presented the process of negotiations between China and Great Britain, as well as principles, with Deng Xiaoping's famous formula 'one country, two systems,' which allowed the incorporation of Hong Kong into the motherland.

These ten chapters not only sum up the research interests of the aforementioned students' conference, but, above all, emphasize the images of emerging issues in China at the beginning of the 21st century. One should not also forget that these pictures have been painted by fascination with China, and the wide range of subjects covered by the issue depicts it greatly.

Łukasz Gacek
Ewa Trojnar

Chapter One

Natalia Ożegalska-Łukasik

Dagongmei in the Context of Rural-urban Migration Processes in Contemporary China

Since the late 1970s, the Chinese state has assumed a leading role in economic development. Deng Xiaoping took measures that boosted economic growth just when he lost faith in the Maoist model of central planning and collectivization, as well as realized that in terms of economic development China was considerably behind both new Asian Tigers (South Korea, Taiwan, Hong Kong, and Singapore) and Western capitalists. Rapid economic growth has legitimized the strategy of export-oriented industrialization, pursued through the open-door policy: export-processing, special economic zones, and incentives for foreign investors. Chinese scholars agreed to this kind strategy, as they perceived it as an application of the "grand international cycle" theory, which, in its fundamental nature, describes capital global search for new, cheap sites for investments.[1]

In a short time, China's economic reforms have resulted in a phenomenon of millions of rural people seeking a better life and economic opportunity in the urban areas. These rural to urban migration flows made an impact on almost every social, economic, and political issue in the People's Republic of China. Migrants represent both agents of change at the places of origin and vital contributors to the economic growth in destination areas. Moreover, through migration peasants not only have become a part of the globalization process, but they also indirectly uncovered the rural and interior areas to its effects.[2] Chinese migrants have

[1] C. Cindy Fan, *China on the Move: Migration, the State, and the Household*, New York: Routledge, 2007, p. 3.

[2] Beatriz Carrillo Garcia, "Rural-Urban Migration in China: Temporary Migrants in Search of Permanent Settlement," *Portal Journal of Multidisciplinary International Studies*, Vol. 1/2, 2004, p. 1.

been the subject of a considerable amount of academic studies of both Chinese and non-Chinese scholars. However, the concerns of women have long been neglected in the studies on migration. Also, the impact of gender on migration patterns and experiences has not received sufficient attention though the number of women among the migrating population is substantial, with conditions in certain parts of China apparently favoring female migration.[3] Works from the gender perspective have in mind the creation of theoretical models that would adequately explain the female migration. Yet the analysis is usually limited to either the 'micro' or 'macro' perspective, which is predominant in the gender studies. The 'macro' viewpoint includes classical categories of social structure, class, economic, and political systems – all in the context of globalization which explains the mechanisms and patterns of migration. Women are described as important elements of the new economy, a system based on the service sector, and the transfer of 'soft' capital, which strengthens the central, and weakens the peripheral areas.[4] In global cities, globalization creates a demand for the migrating workforce. At the same time, the forces placing women in peripheral areas create a supply for workers who can be pushed into such kind of work or sold to do it.[5] *Dagongmei* (i.e. 'factory sisters' or 'working girls') constitute a vivid example of this process.

Another important issue in the works on female migration are the categories of "female slaves" or "slave caste" used by scholars. Women are presented as belonging to an invisible and powerless class of workers serving the strategic sector of global economy. The terms refer to life and work conditions of female migrants who are often kept in isolation from the world outside work, have their free time controlled by authorities, are financially dependent on their employer and/or are often subject to manipulation and threats.[6] The lack of 'class consciousness' in female migrants constitutes them a class in itself.

Many sociologists underline the range of phenomena associated with migration: social exclusion, ghettoization, inability to eliminate the periphery syndrome or to leave the poorly paid work segment are present among migrants and especially among women. Exclusion is often seen as a vicious circle of negative circumstances. Many women do not have

---

[3] Delia Davin, *Internal Migration in Contemporary China*, London: Macmillan Press Ltd, 1999, p. 2.

[4] Marta Smagacz-Poziemska, *Między domem a globalnym rynkiem. Przegląd współczesnych perspektyw i koncepcji w badaniach migrantek na rynku pracy*, in: Krystyna Slany, *Migracje kobiet. Perspektywa wielowymiarowa*, Kraków: Wydawnictwo Uniwersytetu Jagiellońskiego, 2008, p. 37–38.

[5] Saskia Sassen, *Global Networks, Linked Cities*, New York: Routledge, 2002, p. 274.

[6] Smagacz-Poziemska, *op. cit.*, p. 39.

a work permit and, therefore, are exposed to exploitation. Since there are no official laws regulating this issue, they cannot seek justice in courts.

In the studies on migrants the category of social capital becomes useful. It brings into discussion the non-economic and non-political aspects that are deeply rooted in human relationships, and serve the well-being of the community by integrating the individuals, and thus giving them safety and the sense of belonging.[7] Regardless of the macro-social determinants, each migration has a deep and often dramatic impact on the life of an individual that leads to changes in attitudes, reorientation of identity, and the reconstruction of personality in migrants. What is more, even if migration was only temporary and resulted in returning home, the experience causes permanent psychological change.[8] According to Floya Anthias, "migrants are dynamically located in three places: in the society to which they migrated, in their homeland and in the group of migrants."[9]

Floating population vs the *hukou* system

To understand the importance and range of the internal migration in China it is necessary to look back at the previous generation. The Mao era left no room for spontaneous migration, since one of the methods used by the government to monitor the population was the household registration or *hukou* system. Kam Wing Chan and Li Zhang have described it as "one of the major tools of social control used by the state," and as a "part of a larger economic and political system set up to serve multiple state interest."[10] The *hukou* system divided people into four categories, and, therefore, separated the Chinese society into two major groups. The first two categories are associated with a person's place of registration or *hukou suozaidi* (rural or urban), and the other two deal with a person's type of registration or *hukou leibie* (agricultural or non-agricultural).[11] The registration system made a clear distinction between the agricultural and urban labor force, thus creating spatial hierarchies between the citizens of the city and countryside. Furthermore, children born to a mother

[7] *Ibid.*, p. 44–45.

[8] Tadeusz Paleczny, *Migracje*, in: *Słownik społeczny*, ed. by Bogdan Szlachta, Kraków: Wydawnictwo WAM, 2004, p. 662.

[9] Floya Anthias, "Where do I Belong? Narrating Collective Identity and Translocational Positionality," *Ethnicities*, Vol. 2, No. 4, December 2002, p. 500.

[10] Kam Wing Chan and Li Zhang, "The Hukou System and Rural-Urban Migration in China: Process and Changes," *The China Quarterly*, No. 160, 1999, p. 821–822, in: Garcia, *op. cit.*, p. 5.

[11] *Ibid.*, p. 5.

with a rural *hukou* had rural status regardless of their father's registration status. Even children born in a town or a city to an urban father could not acquire an urban status if the mother had a rural *hukou*. Such a child had no right to food rations or schooling in urban areas. These regulations demand further consideration, since in the Chinese patrilineal and patriarchal tradition, a child is normally perceived as belonging to the father's family. Why then the state insists in this case that the child inherits the mother's status? The explanation lies in the state determination to limit the numbers of urban population. It is socially acceptable for men to 'marry down' in the Chinese society, but much less so for the women to do so. Accordingly, 'mixed marriages' between men of high status (urban *hukou*) and women of low status (rural *hukou*) occur more often than between urban women and rural men. Men are also more occupationally 'mobile' than women, and, therefore, are more likely to move up the spatial hierarchy through the state employment system.[12] Such policy proves that the institutional structure of the *hukou* system also reinforced gender inequality, since it is associated with cultural constructs of gender and labor.[13]

Since 1984, when the *Regulations of Permanent Residence Registration* were alleviated, millions of Chinese rural residents have migrated to the urban areas in search of employment. This tendency is increasing, as the income gap between rural and urban areas subsequently becomes larger. Even though the loosening of the traditional *hukou* system allowed rural residents to migrate, it did not allow them to change their residence status or gain any profits in the cities. It resulted in the emergence of an ever-growing population of migrant laborers living in the cities without minimal benefits of residency including medical care, housing or education for their children.[14] Most of these migrants are the so-called unofficial, *de facto* temporary, or non-*hukou* migrants, belonging to what is commonly referred to as the 'floating population.'[15] According to *The 2010 Report on the Development of China's Floating Population*, the estimated size of this group in 2009 was beyond 200 million people.[16] The term 'floating population' was coined with regards to practically anyone who

[12] Davin, *op. cit.*, p. 6.

[13] Arianne M. Gaetano and Tamara Jacka, "Introduction: Focusing on Migrant Women," in: *On the Move: Woman in Rural-to-Urban Migration in Contemporary China*, ed. by Arianne M. Gaetano and Tamara Jacka, New York: Columbia University Press, 2004, p. 21.

[14] *"Dagongmei" – Female Migrant Labourers*, China Labour Bulletin, http://www.china-labour.org.hk/en/node/3448 (May 30, 2011).

[15] Tamara Jacka, *Rural Women in Urban China: Gender, Migration and Social Change*, New York: M.E. Sharp, 2006, p. 7.

[16] "China's 'floating population' exceeds 210m," Xinhua, *China Daily*, June 27, 2010, http://www.chinadaily.com.cn/china/2010-06/27/content_10024861.htm (May 30, 2011).

has moved away, either temporarily or permanently, from their registered place of residence without corresponding transfer of official residence registration. The majority of workforce in China's special economic zones and in other newly industrialized districts are called the *dagongmei*. The approximate size of this group is 50 millions. The following paragraphs are intended to bring a broader description of migration concerning this particular group in the Chinese society.[17]

Dagongmei – who are they?

Since the early 1990s, the development of special economic zones and technology development zones across China was based on a massive exploitation of young workers, in particular of unmarried women who are considered the cheapest and the most obedient workers. *Dagongmei* constitutes new gendered labor group shaped at the particular moment when the private and the international capital appeared in the post-Mao era. Ngai explained that as a newly coined term, *dagongmei* embraces a multi-layered meaning, and denotes a new kind of labor relationship fundamentally different from those from the Mao period. *Dagong* means 'working for the boss' or 'selling labor' which represents commodification and capitalist exchange of labor for wages. This new concept is in contradiction to the Chinese socialist history. Labor, which is evidently emancipated by the Chinese revolution, is again sold to the capitalists, and this time it happens under the auspices of the state. In contrast to the term *gonren*, 'worker,' which denoted the highest status in the socialist rhetoric of Mao's times, the new word *dagong* symbolizes a weakened identity of a hired hand, with a context shaped by the rise of market factors in labor relations and hierarchy. *Mei* means a 'younger sister' (in contrast to *jie*, i.e. an 'older sister'). It implies not just gender, but also marital status – *mei* is unmarried and young, and thus often of a lower status.[18] Nevertheless, Tamara Jacka pointed out as well that the term *dagongmei* paradoxically does not necessarily carry a negative connotation for young women from rural areas, it rather provides new identities and new senses of the self that they acquire once they begin to work in the city.[19]

[17] *On the Move: Woman in Rural-to-Urban Migration...*, p. 19.

[18] Pun Ngai, "Engendering Chinese Modernity: The Sexual Politics of Dagongmei in a Dormitory Labour Regime," *Asian Studies Review*, Vol. 28, June 2004, p. 151.

[19] Tamara Jacka, "Working Sister Answer Back: The Presentation and Self-presentation of Women in China's Floating Population," *China Information*, Vol. 13 (1), 1998, p. 60.

Age and marital status

Age and marital status are important determinants of women's migration in China as elsewhere, although researches are not all in agreement on the exact relationship between these variables, and there is some evidence that the picture is changing over time. To date, most surveys indicated that the migrant population is on average younger than the rural non-migrant population, women tend to be younger and less often married. In general among non-*hukou* migrants, women are concentrated in the 15–19 years old group, whereas men are concentrated in the 20–24 years old cohort.[20] In the scale of the country some 83 percent of female migrant workers are estimated to be under the age of 30, compared to only 55 percent of male migrant workers who are under 30. The precise relations between age and sex of migrants as given by 2000 census were presented on Figure 1.

The difference in ages is a result of several factors. First of all, as married women are less mobile, female migrant workers are younger and more likely to be single than their male counterparts. Young women are generally seen as easier to control than male employees. What is more,

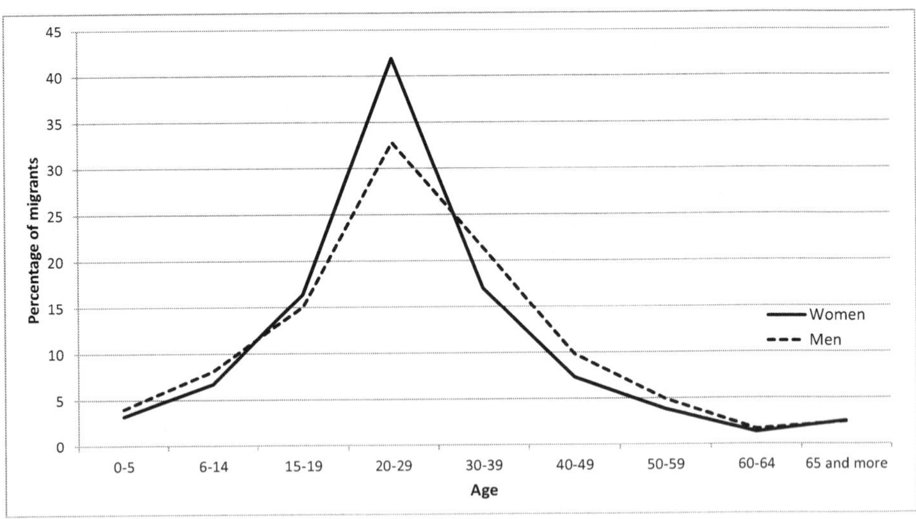

Figure 1. Age and sex of migrants according to the 2000 census

Source: own work based on the data from "Major Figures on 2000 Population Census of China (No. 1)," *National Bureau of Statistics Peoples Republic of China*, March 28, 2001, in: *Women and men in China. Facts and figures 2004*, Beijing: Department of Population, Social Science and Technology, National Bureau of Statistics, August 2004, p. 15.

[20] *On the Move: Woman in Rural-to-Urban Migration...*, p. 23.

such women have little knowledge of their rights. They are less likely to get pregnant, more willing to work long hours. Younger women also have added advantage of being able to endure continual overtime and lack of rest days that many factories offer.[21]

Another important factor which has to be taken into account is the strong tradition and the social pressure for peasant women to marry young. Marriage has two implications for female peasant migrants. First, most women return to the countryside to find their marriage partner. Second, once they are married, and especially after they have children, peasant women usually completely abandon the pursuit of migrant work. Both explain why young, single women are more highly represented than the older, married women among rural labor migrants.[22] The traditional Chinese ideology defined women in reference to marriage, and postulated that marriage. Even the engagement legitimizes the transfer of woman's labor, and autonomy to the future husband's household. The opinion that migrant women are immoral is also related to the age-old belief that woman's proper place is 'inside' (the home and the village). Marriage traditions in rural China – women marrying at a young age, migrant women returning home for marriage, and staying in the village upon marriage – mean that migrant work is nothing but a short episode during a peasant women's youth. It is common that marriage denotes the end of migrant and urban work for a peasant woman.[23]

However, there is also some interesting evidence that the probability of married women migration increases with the birth of a male child. Rural households' desire for a male heir is well documented as a historical and contemporary tendency. The birth of a son may provide his mother with a bargaining power in the household, in particular the ability to demand child care from her in-laws, thus facilitating her own migration.[24]

Education

In rural China, most young women do not continue their education beyond junior secondary school, and many withdraw from school after completing the primary level. The decision to withdraw at or before junior secondary school may be made by themselves or by their parents, but either way it reflects the age-old view that education for the daughter is

[21] *"Dagongmei" – Female Migrant...*

[22] Fan, *op. cit.*, p. 86.

[23] *Ibid.*, p. 88.

[24] *On the Move: Woman in Rural-to-Urban Migration...*, p. 28.

a waste of time and money, because she will eventually marry out and become a member of another household. At the same time, the large agricultural labor excess and lack of farmland mean that many peasant women have never or hardly ever engaged in farming. Those in their late teens after leaving school may have little to do other than house chores. Having 'nothing to do at home' is, indeed, a common explanation by peasant women for their pursuit of migrant work. Young peasant women's quest for migrant work not only brings family financial savings by their 'not eating at home,' but it is also a means of increasing household income, and creating opportunities for others, especially for male siblings.[25]

Migration channels and social networks

In contrast to stereotype, the majority of the floating population does not migrate blindly, but it responds systematically to information channeled to the villages mainly through social networks comprised of relatives and co-villagers. Major flows of migrants reported in the 2000 census are shown in Figure 2. It is noticeable that the main directions of migration are from the western parts of the country to the east coast. The largest group of incoming citizens is concentrated in the Guangzhou province.

Dilemmas of the heart: motivation for migration and *dagongmei's* problems in the cities and workplaces

Generally, migration is characterized by a mixture of push and pull factors, including the economic poverty of home villages, desire to lessen the burden to the family by leaving, and the sense of being unproductive and without value as unmarried daughters. Consequently, on one hand, migration can be regarded as a displacement rather than a positive movement. However, there are also strong pull factors, expressed by these women in phrases such as "to test myself" (*duanlian ziji*), "to open my eyes" (*kaikuo yanjie*) and "to change myself" (*gaibian ziji*). Young rural women leaving for the city seek a sense of independence and value. They recognize the struggle and monotony of their present and future rural lives. Notably, they use migration for work to avoid early marriages, and draw away pressure from parents to control their marriage choices. At the same time, they see such migration as a chance to form a better marriage.

[25] Fan, *op. cit.*, p. 85.

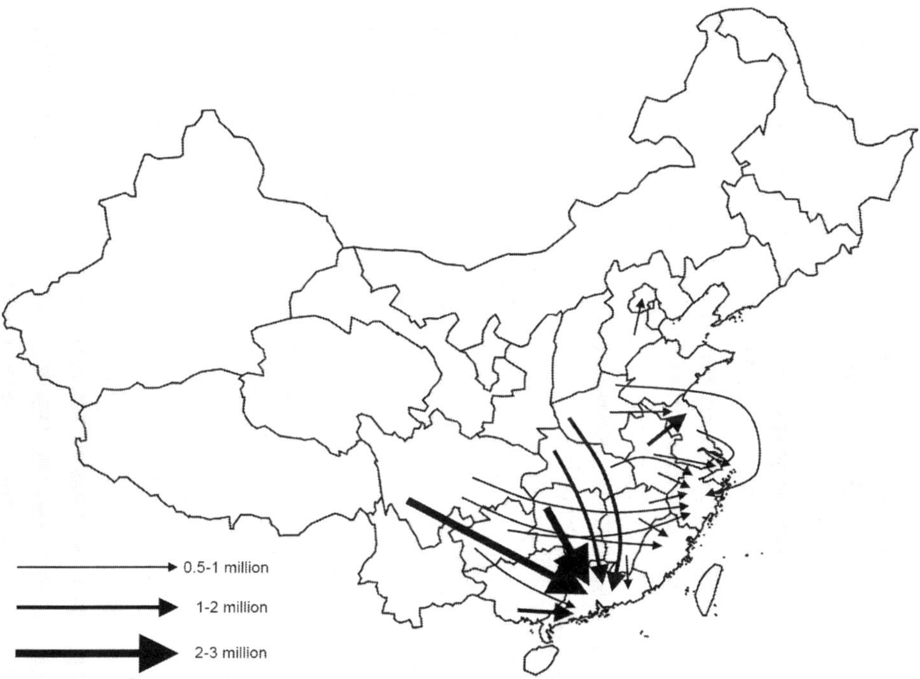

Figure 2. Main directions of interprovincial migration in China in the period 2000–2005, according to the 2005 Sample Survey of 1%

Source: own work based on the data from "2005 nian quanguo 1% renkou chouyang diaocha ziliao (Data on the Sample Survey of 1% of the National Population in 2005)," Zhongguo tongji chubanshe (Chinese Statistics Press), Beijing: State Council, Population Census Office and Department of Population Statistics, State Statistical Bureau, 2007, in: Kam Wing Chan, *China, Internal Migration*, Washington: May 2011, http://faculty.washington.edu/kwchan/Chan-migration.pdf, p. 11. (May 28, 2011).

Thus, alternatively, their migration can be regarded as a positive desire to run away, to gain autonomy, and to change their fate.[26]

Nevertheless, female migrant workers struggle with many problems in the cities, both related to work and to the new place of residence. They are suffering because of health issues and bad safety conditions at work. Each year, thousands of workers are maimed while working on machines without safety guards or in dangerous conditions. This is especially true in smaller privately owned manufacturing enterprises that require their female workers to operate machinery without proper safety guards or maintenance checks. The Chinese Labor Bulletin (CLB) has monitored many cases of fires, chemical spills, explosions, loss of limbs, most of which could have been avoided if there had been proper attention and

[26] Louise Beynon, "Dilemmas of the Heart: Rural Working Women and Their Hopes for The Future," in: *On the Move: Woman in Rural-to-Urban Migration...*, p. 133.

enforcement of existing safety legislation. Thousands of female migrant workers suffer from deadly diseases caused by working in factories laden with chemical fumes or toxic dust. Without the right to form unions, and with only the state sanction of the All China Federation of Trade Union there is little help for workers wanting to protect themselves from unscrupulous employers.[27] Another problem is caused by differences in languages spoken by female workers. China is a big country with numerous dialects. The struggle over regional, rural/urban, and ethnic identities should lead to investigation over the politics of dialects in the workplace. Language is a system of symbols produced and reproduced in the net of social differences, hierarchies, and distinctions which constitute social reality. It does matter what dialect and what accent does one use. In the factory, a hierarchy of dialects was deployed in a 'language war' linked to the struggle over work position, resources, and power. Mandarin is the official language in China, but in much of Guangdong (where most factories are located) it has lost its legitimacy to Cantonese.[28] Several researchers have reported that as a result of such language barrier different local or ethnic groups in the work place may seldom talk to each other and make friends across the boundaries. Discriminatory language used by the city dwellers also appears. Depreciative terms like *xiangxiamei* ('village girl') or *cushou cujiao* ('sun-burned hands') are often used. *Cushou cujiao* is the physical stigma of a peasant, whereas *xiangxiamei* was the abject identity that had to be polished and upgraded.[29] As Pun Ngai reports, distrust is also frequently worsened by the lack of spare time to communicate with coworkers. Daily conflicts sometimes escalate due to tight space and rushed time, aggravated by the mutual creation of negative images. Since the migrant working class is deprived of the right to stay in the city, the state controls labor mobility by dormitory regime.[30] The experience of living in the city is offering *dagongmei* a taste of cosmopolitan lifestyle, and, more importantly, the self affirmation of modern gendered subjects.[31] For them, places like fashion shops, department stores, supermarkets, and coffee houses are manifestations of the Western world. Their consumerism is driven by an urgent desire to reduce the disproportion between themselves and the city dwellers, as well as by an ambition to live up to the calling of a modern model of female beauty, increasingly presented by the mass media. The switch to being

[27] *"Dagongmei" – Female Migrant...*

[28] Ngai, "Becoming Dagongmei (Working Girls): The Politics of Identity and Difference in Reform China," *The China Journal*, No. 42, July 1999, p. 9.

[29] *Ibid.*, p. 5.

[30] Ngai, *Made in China*, Durham and London: Duke University Press, 2005, p. 160–162.

[31] Ngai, "Engendering Chinese Modernity...," p. 162.

a modern woman, even if only in terms of appearances, expresses dreams and desires of *dagongmei* as they strive to transform themselves. It is sad truth that in the urban industrial world the 'lure of consumption' produces irresistible desire to consume, even for those who cannot afford it.[32]

Conclusions

In contemporary China the search for modernity has resulted in opening the socialist economy to global capitalism. At the beginning of the 21st century, China is well known as the 'world factory', attracting transnational corporations from all over the world, especially Hong Kong, Taiwan, Japan, the USA, and the Western Europe. During the first decade of the new millennium, the rise of China was carefully observed by media around the globe. The success of the 2008 Olympic Games in Beijing and the 2010 World Expo in Shanghai showed how rapid the country's development was.

Behind the glamour, millions of migrant workers have been toiling for decades to make, build, and serve. This massive population that flows from rural to urban areas does not only constitute 'the phenomenon of the century' for China, but it also represents the largest flow of labor out of agriculture in the world history.[33] The aim of this short article was to outline the main problems connected with rural-urban migration, drawing special attention to the group formed of young women called the *dagongmei*. The importance of this phenomenon is measured not only by the numbers of women trying to improve their status, but also by their input to the modernization of China, and the impact on the global economy.

Bibliography

"2005 nian quanguo 1% renkou chouyang diaocha ziliao (Data on the Sample Survey of 1% of the National Population in 2005)," Zhongguo tongji chubanshe (Chinese Statistics Press), Beijing: State Council, Population Census Office and Department of Population Statistics, State Statistical Bureau, 2007, in: Kam Wing Chan, *China, Internal Migration*, Washington: May 2011, http://faculty.washington.edu/kwchan/Chan-migration.pdf (May 28, 2011).

[32] *Ibid.*

[33] Garcia, *op. cit.*, p. 1.

Anthias Floya, "Where do I belong? Narrating Collective Identity and Translocational Positionality," *Ethnicities*, Vol. 2, No. 4, December 2002.
Chan Kam Wing and Zhang Li, "The Hukou System and Rural-Urban Migration in China: Process and Changes," *The China Quarterly*, No. 160, 1999.
"China's 'floating population' exceeds 210m," Xinhua, *China Daily*, June 27, 2010, http://www.chinadaily.com.cn/china/2010-06/27/content_10024861.htm (May 30, 2011).
"Dagongmei" – Female Migrant Labourers, China Labour Bulletin, http://www.china-labour.org.hk/en/node/3448 (May 30, 2011).
Delia Davin, *Internal Migration in Contemporary China*, London: Macmillan Press Ltd, 1999.
Fan C. Cindy, *China on the Move, Migration, the State, and the Household*, New York: Routledge, 2007.
Gaetano Arianne M. and Jacka Tamara, "Introduction: Focusing on Migrant Women," in: *On the Move: Woman in Rural-to-Urban Migration in Contemporary China*, ed. by Arianne M. Gaetano and Tamara Jacka, New York: Columbia University Press, 2004.
Garcia Beatriz Carrillo, "Rural-Urban Migration in China: Temporary Migrants in Search of Permanent Settlement," *Portal Journal of Multidisciplinary International Studies*, Vol. 1/2, 2004.
Jacka Tamara, *Rural Women in Urban China: Gender, Migration and Social Change*, New York: M.E. Sharp, 2006.
Jacka Tamara, "Working Sister Answer Back: The Presentation and Self-presentation of Women in China's Floating Population," *China Information*, Vol. 13 (1), 1998.
Louise Beynon, "Dilemmas of the Heart: Rural Working Women and their Hopes for the Future," in: *On the Move: Woman in Rural-to-Urban Migration in Contemporary China*, ed. by Arianne M. Gaetano and Tamara Jacka, New York: Columbia University Press, 2004.
Ngai Pun, "Becoming Dagongmei (Working Girls): The politics of Identity and Difference in Reform China," *The China Journal*, No. 42, July 1999.
Ngai Pun, *Made in China*, Durham and London: Duke University Press, 2005.
Ngai Pun, "Engendering Chinese Modernity: The Sexual Politics of Dagongmei in a Dormitory Labour Regime," *Asian Studies Review*, Vol. 28, June 2004.
Paleczny Tadeusz, *Migracje*, in: *Słownik społeczny*, ed. by Bogdan Szlachta, Kraków: Wydawnictwo WAM, 2004.
Sassen Saskia, *Global Networks, Linked Cities*, New York: Routledge, 2002.
Smagacz-Poziemska Marta, *Między domem a globalnym rynkiem. Przegląd współczesnych perspektyw i koncepcji w badaniach migrantek na rynku pracy*, in: Krystyna Slany, *Migracje kobiet. Perspektywa wielowymiarowa*, Kraków: Wydawnictwo Uniwersytetu Jagiellońskiego, 2008.
Women and men in China. Facts and figures 2004, Beijing: Department of Population, Social Science and Technology, National Bureau of Statistics, August 2004.

Chapter Two

Agnieszka Szajna-Węgrzyn

The Linguistic Features of the Chinese Internet Language

At 338 million, the number of Internet users in China ranks second only to the United States.[1] Moreover, Chinese speakers constitute 29.7 percent of the total of 1.8 billion Internet users worldwide, ranking second to English.[2] However, little is known about how Chinese speakers use language online, in contrast to a large amount of research done on languages that utilize Roman- based script. This article attempts to describe the linguistic and paralinguistic features of informal computer-mediated communication in Chinese. The research is based on a review of existing research and analysis of data massages posted on websites. Throughout the course of the study I aimed to answer the research questions stated below:

- What are the linguistic features of the Chinese Internet language (CIL)?
- Why is the language on the web adopting such a linguistic form?
- Why do Internet users create and use unique language form called the Chinese Internet language?

In order to receive answers to these questions I have based my analysis upon four areas: definition and description of linguistic features of the Chinese Internet language, characteristics of online asynchronous communication, and its functions.

---

[1] *Statistical Report on Internet Development in China (July 2009)*, China Internet Network Information Center, http://www.cnnic.net.cn/uploadfiles/pdf/2009/10/12/114121.pdf, p. 11 (January 29, 2012).

[2] *Internet World Users by Language. Top 10 Languages*, Internet World Stats June 2010, http://www.internetworldstats.com/stats7.htm (January 29, 2012).

Definition of the Chinese Internet language and factors contributing to the emergence of the Internet language

The rapid development of the Internet in China has had a huge impact on the Chinese language. Computer-mediated communication gave rise to a new variety of Chinese that is being called the Chinese Internet language. CIL can be defined either in a broad or a narrow sense. In a broad sense, this term is associated with technical terms related to the Internet language necessary to describe online communication as well as informal expressions created and used by the Internet users in the process of computer-mediated communication. In a narrow sense, the Chinese Internet language means words and phrases employed on the Internet for everyday interaction mainly through chat rooms.[3] CIL was formed under the influence of several factors, such as technical constrains, social conditions, context of communication and users. I will try to discuss these constraints below.

On one hand, the Internet overcame traditional limitations of time and space allowing people from all around the world to exchange information in relatively fast pace. Interaction between interlocutors is often rapid and informal, and hence more like spoken conversation. On the other hand, online dialogue is typed, so the sender and the receiver are traditionally constrained linguistically by the properties of the computer hardware linking them. Because of this fact, the Chinese Internet language is hard to be classified in the traditional division between speech and writing. Language in the Internet is a unique linguistic hybrid combining these elements that is often called a "written speech."[4] Chinese in the Internet is subject to additional restrictions related to the amplification of Chinese characters. There are many ways to edit Chinese characters via the keypad, but each of them is much slower than the record based on the Latin alphabet.

Another factor influencing the form of Chinese in the Internet is the social and cultural background. In opinion of many researchers there is a link between language and cultural context, although the exact nature of this relationship is subject to linguistic discussions. If we assume that language is a mirror of the society then we can perceive CIL as a product of recent social developments in China. Social and political changes that

[3] Liwei Gao, *Chinese Internet Language, Chinese Internet Language. Study of Identity Construction*, Urbana: University of Illinois, 2004, p. 11.; Jianhua Chen, "Wangluo yuyan de fazhan jiqi guifan," in: *Journal of Fuzhou University*, No. 1 (65), 2004, p. 75.

[4] David Crystal, *Language in the Internet*, Cambridge: Cambridge University Press, 2001, p. 27.

have occurred in China since 1978 forced a transformation in a language that has evolved in order to describe those huge changes.[5]

Language use is determined by the context in which the act of communication takes place. The Internet is not a homogenous environment in terms of language use. On the web, you can find communication contexts in which language is very formal. At the same time, however, you can easily come across such a situation, where the language seems to be devoid of any standards. Chat groups are a unique communication environment, where netizens are released from restrictions of conventional language practice. The discourse takes the form similar to speech, and the language is very innovative and informal.[6]

The last factor shaping the language on the web are the Chinese Internet users. According to the report on the development of the Internet in China published by the China Internet Network Information Center, the Internet users are primarily young and well-educated people. Regarding their professional background, they are mainly students, college professors, researchers, and employers of major companies.[7] On the basis of the demographic characteristics given above we can assume that language on the web will be innovative, original, and full of foreign influences.

Linguistic and paralinguistic features of the Chinese Internet language

Possibly one of the most distinctive features of the online Chinese is the way the language is abbreviated in comparison to the standard written Chinese. On the Chinese Internet, two subcategories of acronyms are identified, namely English letter initials and *pinyin* initials. English letter initials refer to the adoption of the first letter in an English phrase. In turn, *pinyin* initials are based on the first *pinyin* of each character in a Chinese phrase.[8] Examples of these abbreviations are given in tables 1 and 2.

---

[5] Gao, *op. cit.*, p. 6–10.

[6] Yuan Zhang, *Guanyu wangluo yuyan*, Wuhan: Wuhan Daxue Zhongwen Xi, 2002, p. 104.

[7] *China Internet Network Information*, http://www.cnnic.net.cn/uploadfiles/pdf/2009/10/12/114121.pdf, p. 16–20 (March 12, 2012).

[8] Chunsheng Yang, *Chinese Internet Language: A Sociolinguistic Analysis of Adaptations of the Chinese Writing System (2007)*, "Language@Internet," Vol. 4, http://nbn-resolving.de/urn:nbn:de:0009-7-11425 (March 12, 2012).

Table 1. List of common English letter initials in the Chinese Internet

Initials	English meaning	Chinese meaning
GF	girlfriend	*nv pengyou*女朋友
BF	boyfriend	*nan pengyou*男朋友
RE	regarding	*guanyu*关于
LOL	laugh out loudly	*da sheng xiao*大声笑

Source: own work based on Jianhua Chen, "Wangluo yuyan de fazhan jiqi guifan," *Journal of Fuzhou University*, No. 1 (65), 2004, p. 76.

Table 2. List of popular *pinyin* initials on the Chinese Internet

Initials	Chinese meaning	English meaning
MM	*meimei* 妹妹	girl
LM	*lamei* 辣妹	spice girl
GG	*gege*哥哥	boy
PLMM	*piaoliang meimei* 漂亮妹妹	beautiful girl

Source: own work based on *Wangluo yuyan cidian (December 2009)*, NetEase, http://news.163.com/09/1205/18/5PPR4J2C000120GR.html (March 12, 2012).

The tendency to create acronyms is the result of the character of communication via chat groups. The dialogues are conducted in a very fast pace, almost as fast as a face to face communication. The interlocutors communicate under a time pressure and the receiver is compelled to provide an instant response. It is possibly the case that the users are constantly forced to think of and find new ways of reducing the number of keystrokes needed at all time. It is also worth noting that creation of initials may also serve as a marker of both group identity and social status in chat rooms[9]. Netizens familiar with abbreviations may freely join the conversation, whereas Internet users who do not know the specific language will be automatically pushed to the margins.

The Chinese Internet users create abbreviations not only on the basis of the first letters of words constituting the phrase, but also with the help of numbers. The number code is based just on the phonetic similarity. Using Arabic numerals in communication is convenient and easy to store and remember, so it is hardly surprising that this process is so popular in the Chinese Internet. Table 2 contains examples of such codes.[10]

[9] Adam Blakeman, *An Investigation of the Language of Internet Chat Rooms*, LING 201 Dissertation, Lancaster: Lancaster University 2004, p. 26–28.

[10] Zhang, *op. cit.*, p. 103.

Table 3. List of popular number initials on the Chinese Internet

Number initials	Chinese meaning	English meaning
7456	*qi si wo le* 气死我了	indignant
9494	*jiu shi jiu shi* 就是就是	that is it
748	*qu si ba*去死吧	go to hell
8147	*bu yao shengqi* 不要生气	don't be angry

Source: own work based on *Wangluo yuyan cidian (December 2009)*, NetEast, http://news.163.com/09/1205/18/5PPR4J2C000120GR.html (March 13, 2012); *Wangluoyuyan (November 2009)*, Baidu wenku, http://wenku.baidu.com/view/1755ec1755270722192ef754.html (April 10, 2010).

Another characteristic of the online language is the use of words and phrases derived from foreign languages, especially English. Examples of foreign interspersion are given below:

- ...可是她觉得张得普普 可能不是女生喜欢的style吧 (*keshi ta juede zhang de pupu keneng bu shi nvsheng xihuan de* style *ba*);
- 大部分作品的idea都是从他来的 (*da bufen zuopin de* idea *dou shi cong ta lai de*);
- 说吧说吧, please (*shuo ba shuo ba);*
- 感觉她是一个很nice的人 (*ganjue ta shi yi ge hen* nice *de ren).*[11]

The reason for adding English words or expressions is a desire to emphasize one's language skills and high status in the group. What is more, English expressions impart an international character to the online discourse as well as express the sender's will to be perceived as a worldly person open to the world.

Internet users not only borrow English words and phrases but also create original stylizations by using Chinese characters to record sounds of English. The Chinese writing system is used only to mark the pronunciation, whereas the original meaning of characters is completely ignored. The use of stylized forms shows a creative approach to language, as well as expresses the netizens' pride of the traditional writing system that significantly distinguishes them from the Internet users living in other parts of the world. Stylized English reduces stiffness and arrogance often linked with the Chinese people's use of foreign language, giving this linguistic practice a sense of locality, and simultaneously indicating that the users possess a highly valued linguistic competence.[12]

[11] Luqun Ge, *An Investigation on English/Chinese Code-switching in BBS in Chinese Alumni's Community*, Edinburgh: The University of Edinburgh, 2007, http://hdl.handle.net/1842/1937 (March 12, 2012).

[12] In this context by the *stylized representations* we understand the use of the Chinese characters to represent the linguistic varieties other than Mandarin: Hsi-Yao Su, *The Multi-Orthographic Taiwan-Based Internet: Creative Uses of Writing Systems on College-Affiliated BBSs*, Austin: University of Texas at Austin, p. 10–12.

Some examples of stylized English are given below:

- *ku* 酷, 'cool';
- *fensi* 粉丝 'fans';
- *fente* 分特 'faint'.[13]

In the Chinese Internet language, there is also vocabulary created on the basis of Mandarin Chinese. This category comprises lexical items which did not exist in Mandarin before or have a totally different meaning in the Internet Chinese.[14] Table 4 contains examples of such words.

Table 4. List of popular Mandarin stylized vocabulary

Chinese Internet language	Literal meaning in Chinese	English meaning
konglong 恐龙	dinosaur	bad-looking girl
cainiao 菜鸟	fresh bird	novice Internet user
qingwa 青蛙	black frog	unattractive male
shanzhai 山寨	village in the mountains	low-quality goods

Source: own work based on *Wangluoyuyan (November 2009)*, Baidu wenku, http://wenku.baidu.com/view/1755ec1755270722192ef754.html (April 10, 2010).

Another visible form of linguistic creativity on the Internet is the use of the stylized dialect-accented Mandarin. In these linguistic practices, adopted characters represent the pronunciation of a dialectal form. Two examples of this stylized representations are given in Table 5.

As it is widely known, there are many dialects of Chinese in the PRC, so it is inevitable for the Internet language to be influenced by these different language varieties. The reference to dialects is not due to the lack of linguistic knowledge, but can be perceived by the netizens as a way to stand out from the Internet crowd.

The Chinese Internet language is missing some paralinguistic cues natural for a face-to-face communication, such as sound and body signal. To compensate for this disadvantage, the netizens create and use many paralinguistic expressions such as emoticons. Emoticons (popularly known as smileys) are sideways representations of face or posture created by keystrokes, and used to communicate emotional states and attitude towards

[13] Yang, *op. cit.*, p. 9.
[14] *Ibid.*, p. 9; Su, *op. cit.*, p. 21–22.

Table 5. Examples of stylized-accented Mandarin vocabulary

Chinese Internet language	Meaning in Mandarin Chinese	English meaning	Origins
ou 偶	*wo* 我	I, my, me	Ningbo dialect
huichang 灰常	*feichang* 非常	Very	northern dialect

Source: own work based on Chunsheng Yang, *Chinese Internet Language: A Sociolinguistic Analysis of Adaptations of the Chinese Writing System (2007)*, "Language@Internet," Vol. 4, http://nbn-resolving.de/urn:nbn:de:0009-7-11425, p. 8 (March 12, 2012).

the speaker.[15] Smileys prevalent in the Chinese Internet significantly differ from emoticons popular in Poland. Traditionally, Chinese smileys are arranged vertically and focus on eyes, whereas emoticons appearing in Europe are written from left to right and focus the attention on the entire face.[16] Emoticons popular in China can be divided into two groups: signs showing facial expressions and those representing gestures and postures. Examples of the use of these paralinguistic signs are given in Table 6.

Table 6. Examples of emoticons

Emoticons	Meaning in Chinese and in English	Remarks
^-^	微笑 *wei xiao*; smiling, happy	emoticons showing facial expressions
^o^	大笑 *da xiao*; very happy	
XD	Smiling, extremely happy	
Orz[17]	Emoticon expresses loss, bad mood, and despair. In a certain context can also mean admiration for another person. The shape resembles a person kneeling. "O" symbolizes the head, "r" shoulders and "z" the rest of the body.	emoticons representing gestures and postures

Source: own work based on *Emoticon*, Wikipedia: http://en.wikipedia.org/wiki/Emoticon (April 10, 2010).

[15] *Smiley* (2007), Dictionary of American Slang and Colloquial Expressions by Richard A. Spears, Fourth Edition, McGraw Hill 2007 on Dictionary.com, http://dictionary.reference.com/browse/smiley (March 13, 2012); Jan Grzenia, *Komunikacja językowa w Internecie*, Warszawa: Wydawnictwo Naukowe PWN, 2006, p. 137.

[16] Judith Burns, "Facial expressions 'not global,'" *BBC*, August 14, 2009, http://news.bbc.co.uk/2/hi/science/nature/8199951.stm (January 29, 2012).

[17] Xeni Jardin, *All about Orz*, Boingboing, February 2005, http://www.boingboing.net/2005/02/07/all-about-orz.html (March 13, 2012).

Functions of the Chinese Internet language

The Chinese Internet language is not only attributable to such factors as constraints imposed by computers as a medium of communication, but also to the netizens' desire to build a certain personal identity, such as being fashionable and cool, being interesting and entertaining, being internationally oriented and transnational.[18] As in other places in the world, keeping up with the latest fashion and being perceived as a cool person is the goal of many young people. The use of the Internet language has become a part of self-image creation, almost as important as clothes and behavior. The netizens gain a *fashionable identity* by using words from foreign languages and creating stylized linguistic forms.[19] The trend of the young people to rebel against the existing rules has also been reflected in the language of the Internet. *Internationally oriented and transnational identity* may be built by the use of stylized-dialectal vocabulary and uncommon language structures.[20] In the era of globalization, *internationally-oriented and transnational identity* has become a very popular trend. In China, English is one of the symbols of internationalization, so this unique personal identity may be created by the use of foreign words and phrases.[21]

Conclusions

This article is an attempt to bring the issue of the Chinese language on the Internet. During the course of my research, I was trying to outline the key features of the language on the web, and answer the question why netizens create and use this unique variety of language.

First reflection which has arisen from the analysis is that the language on the web is heavily abbreviated, full of foreign influences, and innovative. The unique feature of online Chinese is producing three main types of linguistic stylizations based on English, creative use of Mandarin and Chinese dialects. Another characteristic is the popularity of paralinguistic and graphic features, such as emoticons. Secondly, another conclu-

[18] Gao, *op. cit.*, p. 7. Liwei Gao distinguished six different types of identity: a fashionable and cool identity, an interesting and entertaining identity, an unconventional and rebellious, internationally oriented and transnational, a knowledgeable and technologically advanced identity, a young, fresh, and innocent identity.

[19] *Ibid.*, p. 72–73.

[20] *Ibid.*, p. 76–77.

[21] *Ibid.*, p. 79.

sion which can be drawn from the analysis is the fact that the language on the Internet is shaped by many different factors, such as technical constraints, communication context, social and cultural background, as well as users themselves. Thirdly, the Chinese netizens employ a unique language variety, CIL, not only to deal with constraints of the medium, but also in order to establish their distinctive identities, defined as being fashionable and cool, being unconventional and rebellious, as well as being internationally oriented and transnational. Furthermore, the linguistic and paralinguistic analysis has revealed that the Chinese Internet language is a new variety of Chinese, which combines the characteristics of both written and spoken language. This new form of language is increasingly popular in everyday communication and potentially may have an impact on the standard Mandarin Chinese. Considering these matters, much more attention should be paid to the analysis of this linguistic phenomenon.

Bibliography

Blakeman Adam, *An Investigation of the Language of Internet Chat Rooms*, LING 201 Dissertation, Lancaster: Lancaster University, 2004.

Burns Judith, "Facial expressions 'not global,'" *BBC*, August 14, 2009, http://news.bbc.co.uk/2/hi/science/nature/8199951.stm (January 29, 2012).

Chen Jianhua, "Wangluo yuyan de fazhan jiqi guifan," *Journal of Fuzhou University*, No. 1 (65), 2004.

China Internet Network Information, http://www.cnnic.net.cn/uploadfiles/pdf/2009/10/12/114121.pdf (March 12, 2012).

Crystal David, *Language in the Internet*, Cambridge: Cambridge University Press, 2001.

Gao Liwei, *Chinese Internet Language, Chinese Internet Language. Study of Identity Construction*, Urbana: University of Illinois, 2004.

Ge Luqun, *An Investigation on English/Chinese Code-switching in BBS in Chinese Alumni's Community*, Edinburgh: The University of Edinburgh, 2007, http://hdl.handle.net/1842/1937 (March 12, 2012).

Grzenia Jan, *Komunikacja językowa w Internecie*, Warszawa: Wydawnictwo Naukowe PWN, 2006.

Internet World Users by Language. Top 10 Languages, Internet World Stats June 2010, http://www.internetworldstats.com/stats7.htm (January 29, 2012).

Jardin Xeni, *All about Orz*, Boingboing, February 2005, http://www.boingboing.net/2005/02/07/all-about-orz.html (March 13, 2012).

Smiley (2007), Dictionary of American Slang and Colloquial Expressions by Richard A. Spears, Fourth Edition, McGraw Hill 2007 on Dictionary.com, http://dictionary.reference.com/browse/smiley (March 13, 2012).

Statistical Report on Internet Development in China (July 2009), China Internet Network Information Center, http://www.cnnic.net.cn/uploadfiles/pdf/2009/10/12/114121.pdf (January 29, 2012).

Su Hsi-Yao, *The Multi-Orthographic Taiwan-Based Internet: Creative Uses of Writing Systems on College-Affiliated BBSs*, Austin: University of Texas at Austin.

Yang Chunsheng, *Chinese Internet Language: A Sociolinguistic Analysis of Adaptations of the Chinese Writing System (2007)*, "Language@Internet," Vol. 4, http://nbn-resolving.de/urn:nbn:de:0009-7-11425 (March 12, 2012).

Zhang Yuan, *Guanyu wangluo yuyan*, Wuhan: Wuhan Daxue Zhongwen Xi, 2002.

Chapter Three

Michał Witek

Chinese Contemporary Art: Between Market and Freedom

It was something to be expected a few years ago. In the wake of the booming Chinese economy, the Chinese art market would take off sooner or later. It is not only the matter of visual and modern arts, the phenomenon is encompassing the entire cultural sphere in China. Some ask the question is the Chinese art dead or indeed is it really being reborn after years of vegetation under the communist rule, and if so, to what form? To answer this question we must first analyze the phenomenon called the Chinese contemporary art, on the grounds of its history and present. We must furthermore ask a very important question about art in general. This question has been tormenting researchers from at least the beginning of the 20th century. Is art understood as creation of art works, looking for answers, trying to express feelings and emotions, is this notion gone and what replaced it? Is art really being produced now, like any other market commodity, to be sold out? In China, this questions are even more complicated. Some argue that there could be no art without freedom, that art is freedom. But is it really so easy to define this most complex of notions?

The beginning of "Chinese contemporary art"

At the beginning of the 20th century, China entered a new era in its long history. The first decades of this century marked the end of the tradition-bound and inefficient Qing Empire. This transition was violent, a revolution and war forcefully entered China into the modern age. Foreign influences, till now restricted to a handful of ports and diplomatic concessions, flooded China like an irresistible tide. This is the most significant difference between the 20th century and the previous periods of the Chinese history. Indeed, this 'new era' will be defined by this constant influx of foreign ideas and products to China. This is also the moment of the birth of the phenomenon we will call the 'Modern Chinese Art' (*Zhongguo Dangdai Yishu*). For Chinese artists this very moment was the turning point of perhaps the longest continuous art tradition in the world. For the first time the Chinese art so far confined by convention and restricted by tradition took a new, fresh breath. The term 'Chinese art tradition' is a most complicated notion. It is impossible to even try to explain it in the frames of this article. Suffice it to say that this tradition was extremely different from anything in the west. This statement is not only about the matter of aesthetics which is different by nature. The very foundation, the idea behind art in China and in the West was different. To define it we forst need to provide a certain definition of art as something universal to all human cultures. The notion of art is usually understood as a process of deliberately arrangement of items (often with symbolic significance) in a way that influences and affects one or more of the senses, emotions, and intellect. It encompasses a diverse range of human activities, creations, and modes of expression. And the primary source of inspiration was the world itself, the nature. The nature of art was described by Wollheim as "one of the most elusive of the traditional problems of human culture."[1] The Encyclopedia Britannica provides us with the following definition: "the use of skill and imagination in the creation of aesthetic objects, environments, or experiences that can be shared with others."[2] In other words what is most universal about art is that it is natural to humankind. Humans create art in response to an essential need of communication and expression; on a certain level it might be considered the basic repercussion of our intellect, and our inherent ability to create signs, representations, and approximations. However, in the Western tradition, art was always associated with the artist, with an individual. Following the Greek tradition of mimetic art, artists in the West seek to recreate the harmony and beauty of nature. The ideas that define the western art are: 'truth' and 'beauty,' the pursuit of whom was the engine of creation behind all artistic expressions. Western art is also obsessed with names of artist, with the fame that artistic craft and skills brought to the artists. It allowed the Western artists to progress further, to seek out new ways of artistic expression, and the art itself to remain dynamic. In China the situation was different. Art is understood as a craft

[1] Richard Wollheim, *Art and its objects*, Cambridge University Press, 1980, p. 1–2 edn.

[2] „Art," *Britannica Encyclopedia internet edition*, http://www.britannica.com/EBchecked/topic/630806/art/ (February 2, 2012).

that has only one purpose, to enable the artists to achieve a greater perfection in their art, and by doing so to get closer to the Confucian ideal of *wen ren*. Artists also seek to recreate the beauty of nature, but not to do it literally, rather to try to interpret it, and see the truth behind it, and by doing so become closer to the soteriological ideal. In all Chinese philosophical traditions this pursuit is similar, although the goal might be different. That is why, when someone achieved certain degree of mastery, they were immediately followed by a great number of people who would try to emulate their style and methods. In China the greatest mastery is not to be individual, ingenious, but to copy the master's style completely. That is the reason why the Chinese art confined itself to rigid tradition, and following strict guidelines of a certain style. Throughout the century-long history, this rigid tradition rarely, if ever, changed and adapted. This is why the meeting of both Western and Chinese art traditions was so turbulentand, difficult, but also incredibly productive and unique. This is perhaps the sole case in the history of mankind when two fully developed and alien art traditions meet, and to some degree merge.

Chinese defeat in the Sino-Japanese war (1894–1895) produced a massive response from the intellectuals of that time. It spurred a movement for reform among the members of the scholarly class with the ideal of marrying the "Chinese essential principles with Western practical knowledge."[3] It was later called The New Culture Movement (*Xin Wenhua Yundong*). In its final years the Qing dynasty did make some feeble efforts to modernize the country, but those reforms came too late and with too little strength. After the Empire finally collapsed in 1911, the newly formed Republic of China struggled to survive, between foreign powers interfering in Chinese matters and internal political instability. The minister of education declared the "the aesthetics should replace religion."[4] This slogan started an intense effort to modernize the Chinese art tradition, also by adopting the western approach. In the following years between 1911 and the late 1930s, Chinese art was being rethought and reborned as something new.

Many artists, especially painters travelled to Europe to study foreign technics. They brought back Western ideas and Western art. Most artists were fascinated by the freedom of thought and creation, and soon they started to seek a way to integrate this new art into their native tradition. This was the period when photography, cinema, and abstract painting arrived to China. As exemplified by Fu Baoshi (1904–1965) and Zhang Daqian (1899–1983), both of whom studied in Japan and traveled abroad late

[3] See: Julia F. Andrews, and Kuiyi Shen, *A Century in Crisis: Modernity and Tradition in the Art of Twentieth-Century China*, New York: Guggenheim Museum, 1998.

[4] Li Zehou, *The Chinese Aesthetic Tradition*, University of Hawaii Press, 2010, p. 213.

in their lives, some influential artists created hybrid styles that reflected a cosmopolitan attitude toward art, and a willingness to modify inherited traditions through the incorporation of foreign idioms and techniques. Zhang, who became the leading connoisseur and collector, based his diverse painting styles on the firsthand study of early masterpieces, while Fu, an academic, learned about earlier works from reproductions and copies. This early period was the time of an extraordinary freedom, new Chinese art grew up very quickly. It is important to note, that in accordance with the historical background provided above, scholars have very diverse opinions about when Modern Chinese Art truly started. Some will place this in the late Qing period, some after the First Opium War (when photography was introduced to China), some around the beginning of the 20th century, and the May Fourth Movement (*Wu Si Yundong*).[5]

Chinese contemporary art in the Maoist period 1949–1975

Unfortunately this freedom was cut short by the turbulent times of the second Sino-Japanese war, and the subsequent communist revolution. With the establishment of the People's Republic of China in 1949, a new chapter for the Chinese art history started. Again marked by an influx of foreign ideology, but this time of a very different nature. Artistic freedom ended, with the introduction of social realism art paradigm. The Communist Party of China would have full control of the government with Mao Zedong heading the country. The art was presented in a manner that favored the government and communist ideas. Art was designed to serve the propaganda and help to establishing socialism. Artists were heavily promoted when cooperating with the regime, and vice versa, any clash with communist party beliefs would force the artists to become 're-educated' through work on a farm in some distant part of the country. Naturally, all Western ideas and innovations, previously so important, were forbidden and rejected as 'contaminating' elements of imperialistic ideology. Very much like in other communist countries, native art was used as a tool of 'socialist education.' Especially traditional Chinese painting was being heavily promoted, as long as it was useful for the Party. This regime was considerably relaxed in 1953, and after the "Hundred Flowers Campaign" (*Baihua Yundong*) of 1956–1957, traditional Chinese painting experienced a significant revival.

[5] Chow Tse-Tsung, *The May Fourth Movement. Intellectual Revolution in Modern China*, Cambridge/Massachusetts: Harvard University (Harvard East Asian Studies, 6.), xvii, 1960, p. 486.

To some extent, the traditional Chinese art paradigm, as described above, was suitable for the communist purposes. It was not innovative, and sought to improve the artist and the recipients, which was precisely what the socialist art was supposed to do. What were most important in the old Chinese art were the technique and skill, not freedom and individualism. The subject of an art piece was secondary to the process of creation. Therefore, it was a quite natural transition for Chinese painters to depict farmers, workers and the 'New China' instead of mountains and flowers. And even if they wanted to practice the 'old ways,' painting mountains and flowers was not harmful, and in any way politically dangerous for the party. In such art, there is no place for allegory and subterfuge, the art is just a recreation, it speaks in simple words. Social realism art from different countries, especially from the USRR was also being imported and used as a template for the Chinese artists. The climax of this period was undoubtedly the time of the 'Cultural Revolution' (from 1966 through 1976). In this turbulent time all artistic activity ceased. There was an overhaul of many of the arts, with the intention of producing new and innovative art that reflected the benefits of a socialist society. As a part of this, many artists, whose work was deemed to be bourgeois or anti-socialist, were persecuted and prevented from working.[6] Under the slogan: "Destruction of the Four Olds" (*si jiu*):[7] old customs, old culture, old habits, and old ideas, old art also identified as anti-revolutionary was being violently destroyed. Not much survived this terrible catastrophe, including many artists who could continue the art tradition.

Second opening and the period of reforms

The new beginning was not to be expected until the end of the 1970s. Mao Zedong's death in 1975 did not end the period of repressions. Another five years had to pass in order for the new lasting government to establish itself. Some place the rebirth of the Chinese art together with Deng Xiaoping's (1904–1997) policy of opening China to the West in 1979.[8] The following period will become known as even more productive and dynamic than the beginning of the century. And it bears many similarities to the time of the New Culture Movement. There are some scholars arguing

[6] Gao Mobo, *The Battle for China's Past: Mao and the Cultural Revolution*, London: Pluto Press, 2008, p. 134.

[7] Law Kam-yee, *The Chinese Cultural Revolution Reconsidered: beyond purge and Holocaust*, 2003, p. 223.

[8] Melissa Chiu, *Chinese Contemporary Art: 7 Things You Should Know*, New York: AW Asia, 2008, p. 112.

that this was the only truly 'free' period in the Chinese art history[9] and that it ended in 1989 together with the Tiananmen Square events. For the sake of the argument it is worth mentioning that the decade between 1979 and 1989 was certainly unprecedented in the Chinese cultural history so far and so intense that it is also known as the time of the 'Cultural Fever' (*wenhua re*). Artists who had formerly gone underground with individual endeavors began to re-surface they emerged one after another. And thanks to the government policy of modernizing China, a river of ideas, cultural and intellectual achievements from the west started to flow into the Chinese mainstream.

This time described as "nationwide discussion on subjects such as culture, tradition, modernity, art and particularly the meaning and implication of Western theories,"[10] has emerged in China in the heyday of the reform program changing the Chinese reality on every level from culture to economy. Again in a brief moment China was being rethought and reorganized into something new. This is also the time of the birth of Chinese avant-garde art, often described in the West as Contemporary Chinese Art (*Zhongguo Dangdai Yishu*). This sudden freedom was a reflection of Deng Xiaoping's ambition to incorporate China into the world not only on the economic but also on symbolic front.[11] There are some who argue this was a deliberate move of the Party leaders to create a new commodity, Chinese art as something that could be sold out to the West. The best known examples of the avant-garde are in the field of literature, the 'Xungen movement' (*Xungen Wenxue*) with such magnificent artists as Gao Xingjian, Bei Dao, Su Tong, Jia Pingwa, and Han Shaogong, is considered one of the most important phenomenona in the Chinese cultural history. Literature is very important because it is the primary conduit through which the achievements of Western theorists and artists were being absorbed. In this period contemporary Chinese art fully incorporated painting, film, video, photography, and performance.

Until recently, art exhibitions deemed controversial were routinely shut down by the police, and performing artists in particular faced the threat of arrest in the early 1990s. More recently, the Chinese government has been more tolerant, though many internationally acclaimed artists are still restricted from media exposure at home or have exhibitions ordered closed. Government tolerance was so great that it allowed some

[9] Ralph Croizier, *When Was Modern Chinese Art? A Short History of Chinese Modernism*, in: *Writing Modern Chinese Art: Historiographic Explorations*, ed. by Josh Yiu, Seattle: Seattle Art Museum and University of Washington Press, 2009, p. 154.

[10] Zhang Xudong, *On Some Motifs in the Chinese „Cultural Fever" of the Late 1980s, Social Change, Ideology and Theory*, No. 39, Summer 1994, Duke University Press, p. 129.

[11] *Ibid*.

artists to openly address the damage done by the Cultural Revolution, albeit cautiously. The movement was called the 'scar painting' (*shanghen yishu*) and 'the art of the wounded.'[12] By the mid-1980s, boldly experimental and political works were being created in several places around China. This is important because even today the Communist Party of China has never officially allowed any discussion, not to mention a condemnation of the Cultural Revolution; to some extent it is considered a taboo. This shows how deep the transformation of the Chinese art of that time really was. Naturally, the government would not tolerate just anything. In the mid 1980s, when avant-garde movements were at their height, the Party launched an Anti-Spiritual Pollution Campaign in 1983, which was aimed directly against too liberal artistic circles. In reality this move was a result of a dangerous spread of ideas among the Chinese populace. One thing is to tolerate the discourse about new ideas among the thin layer of artists and intellectuals, quite another to allow it to engage a broader public. That is one thing that has always been very characteristic about the internal policy of the Party.

Chinese contemporary art after Tiananmen events in 1989

In a way the Tiananmen Square in 1989, was a direct consequence of this amazing decade. Artists, especially musicians, were very active in student movements, and then on the square. This, among other things, brought the Party to perceive art as something dangerous and subversive, and to introduce drastic measures immediately after the Tiananmen events. For the next three years up to 1992, artist and art were being closely watched, and in a way reverted to the social realist state.

In the years to come, the situation changed completely. Fortunately for China the reforms were not abandoned, and the Chinese economy, together with Chinese influence and importance grew exponentially. In the 1990s, China was already on a steady path to become a superpower in the next century. At this point, the economy was of a pivotal importance, because economic progress soon became the main legitimacy for the party rule, and the main purpose of China. This had to affect art as well as the artists. Art critic Gao Minglu sees the change from the politically motivated 'art of the wounded' to consumerism and leisure after the crack-down on protesters in Tiananmen Square.[13] The rapid economic

[12] Cathryn Meurer, "Move over Mao: Do China's Artists Serve a New Master?," *CNN*, http://www.cnn.com/SPECIALS/1999/china.50/inside.china/art.overview/ (February 2, 2012).

[13] Dieter Wanczura, "Booming Chinese Art Market," *Artelino*, February 2007, http://www.artelino.com/articles/booming-chinese-art-market.asp (February 2, 2012).

changes of the 1990s gave the contemporary artists new themes – the desire to get rich quickly, the competitiveness, the widening gap between rich and poor, consumerism, and leisure. The collision of capitalist and communist ideologies also led to the Political Pop and Cynical Realism style.[14] Another interesting phenomenon of the post-Tiananmen period was the so-called 'Academic Art' (*Xueshu Yishu*).[15] This peculiar kind of art combines classical Chinese techniques with socialist thought and employs Western modern art styles such as impressionism and cubism. Paintings feature landscapes, peasant girls, exotic locations, and little social or political criticism. A multitude of artists start to make their way on the art stage. Among them were the interesting and charismatic figures like Ai Wei Wei, Cai Guo-Qiang, Fang Lijun or Huang Yan. All of them are prominent and interesting artists, but unlike before also good managers and merchants. In the newly established art districts in major cities, they own their own galleries and 'produce' art on a massive scale. These days China's leading avant-garde artists have morphed into multimillionaires who show up at exhibitions wearing Gucci and Ferragamo.

Today, the market for Chinese art, both antique and contemporary, is reported to be among the hottest and fastest-growing in the world, attracting buyers from all over the world.[16] In fact, it is growing so fast that some experts suspect it might be showing symptoms of overheating by now.[17] According to the Sotheby's (the biggest auction house in the world) report for 2011, Chinese contemporary art is the most sought after in the world.[18] In 2007, five out of ten bestselling artists in the world were from China, with artists such as Zhang Xiaogang whose works were sold for a total of 56.8 million USD at an auction in 2007.[19] Already in the year 2000 China overtook France and become the world's third largest art market, loosing only to the USA and Japan. Today many of the leading and most influential merchants are from China or Hong Kong. In fact, Hong Kong is becoming an increasingly popular art-buying destination, establishing itself as the most important art market hub in the world. During the global economic crisis, the contemporary Asian art market

---

[14] *Ibid.*

[15] Dangdai Yishu Huigui Xueshu Yishu Shi Cheng, "Jingji Zhibiao," *Jichu*, January 6, 2011, http://arts.cul.sohu.com/20110106/n278707426.shtml (February 2, 2012).

[16] David Barboza, "Booming Chinese Art Market – Report," *The New York Times*, January 4, 2007.

[17] "Going, going, up. Easy money is pouring into the modern-art world," *The Economist*, January 11, 2007, http://www.economist.com/node/8522411 (February 2, 2012).

[18] "Form 10-Q for SOTHEBYS," *Quarterly Report*, November 9, 2011, http://biz.yahoo.com/e/111109/bid10-q.html (February 2, 2012).

[19] Barboza, "Some Contemporary Chinese Artists Are Angry About an April Auction at Sotheby's," *The New York Times*, May 7, 2008.

and the contemporary Chinese art market experienced a slowdown in late 2008. But overall this was a minor setback, and did not affect the Chinese position.[20] Western galleries, especially in Europe, are rushing to sign up unknown painters; artists a year out of college are selling photographic works for as much as 10 thousand USD each; well-known painters have yearlong waiting lists; and the Solomon R. Guggenheim Museum and the Pompidou Center in Paris are considering opening branches in China.

Currently the art market is enormously profitable. As long as the art does not come into the direct path of the Chinese policy, it is only an important element of the state economy. Prestige seems to be a very important element as well. Chinese modern art has become one of the most efficient tools of state propaganda both inside and outside of China. It is extensively used to promote China as a modern and indeed very liberal country. Art helps to build the image of a new China in the 21th century, as an empire not only on the fields of economy or military power but also culture.

Art market situation – characteristics and problems

The contemporary Chinese art market is full of paradoxes and problems. Among them is the question: "where is the Chinese art really going?" Considering the size and importance of this market and the presence of prolific and influential artists, the answer may seem simple. But this is only a matter of perception. The market is growing so fast that the risk of collapse and recession is very high. The current boom in contemporary Chinese art in the view of many experts bears all signs of a bubble. Large collectors who bought Chinese art a few years ago for "an apple and an egg", and art dealers active in the current Chinese art market, will of course not speak of a bubble. Their statements influence the market, and they would be fools to predict a coming collapse or admit exaggerations.[21] Another problem is how much of the original avant-garde art remained. From its birth at the beginning of the century till the 1990s, modern Chinese art was more a revolutionary and meaningful voice, calling for freedom and individualism, fighting against all odds. But today, it is more

[20] James Pomfret, "Chinese Art Sales Weak in Sotheby's HK Auction," *Reuters*, October 8, 2008, http://www.reuters.com/article/2008/10/08/us-art-china-sothebys-idUSTRE4972LU20081008 (February 2, 2012).

[21] Dieter Wanczura, "CNN on the Chinese Market of Contemporary Art," *Artelino*, February 2007, http://www.artelino.com/articles/booming-chinese-art-market.asp (February 2, 2012).

like a product, something that is fueling the Chinese constant economic growth rather than the minds of the Chinese people.

In these contexts, it seems very interesting that many foreign collectors, spending great deal of money on the Chinese art, are indeed looking for this revolutionary and anti-regime spirit, of authenticity and truth. Instead they get what was designed to be suitable for them and to meet their tastes. An interesting thing among Chinese is also the rebirth of the native collecting tradition. In old China collecting the works of art was considered to be very refined and was quite popular among the Confucians. They collected many things ancient Chinese bronze vessels, calligraphy and porcelain were the most popular. With time this tradition rose to the position of an independent art specialty, but was either forgotten or removed after the fall of the Empire. Today with the flourish of the art market, collecting returns as a hobby among rich Chinese.

Another matter is the question of the government control over the Chinese art. For understandable reasons it is quite tight. Government's 'art policy' if such a term might be applied to describe this, is based on two principles: watch artists closely and control the discourse about art inside China. Though a valuable commodity, Chinese experimental art is still struggling, to say the least, for basic acceptance at home. Although books and magazines about avant-garde art are readily available in bookstores, actual exhibitions, especially those involving performances, installation, video, and computer art are still generally discouraged by the official establishment, including state-run art galleries and schools. There has been, in fact, a tighter control over such exhibitions in the past two to three years; as a result at least 10 exhibitions of experimental art in Beijing alone, including five large shows each featuring 20 to 40 artists, were cancelled or early terminated. The reasons behind these cancellations and early terminations are complex. One main reason is the government's frustration in seeing its control over the art world slip. As the cadres in the Ministry of Cultural Affairs and the Ministry of Propaganda face growing difficulties in stopping the flow of information about Western art and ideas, and as they find their own exhibitions attracting fewer and fewer people, they react aggressively to tighten their grasp over those areas they believe are still under their control. Art exhibitions are one such an area. According to a government regulation, all public art exhibitions must be organized by institutions entitled to do so, and all public art exhibitions must be held in registered exhibition spaces, and be approved by responsible authorities. This regulation gives the government and its agencies – the Department of Cultural Affairs or the police – almost unlimited power to turn down any proposed exhibition or to close down any exhibition that has already been installed or even opened: innumerable reasons, from an incomplete approval procedure to an inappropriate exhibition space, can be used to justify such actions.[22] If an independent curator or art gallery owner wants to promote an artist and organize an exhibition, they must face a difficult reality. The amount of bureaucratic restrictions is enormous and if such an event should succeed, the control over this endeavor would be very tight. Fortunately there are still many artists and curators who are willing to try, even if the content of the exhibition will obviously be blocked. That is a good sign for the future of art in China. This attitude of the government shows clearly that the Party is still afraid of the stirring potential of art, and will not allow any discussion about it to leave certain circles. Even if an artist is well known and well selling, like for example Ai Wei Wei, the Party will not hesitate to silence them if only their art poses any threat.

Conclusions

The quality and creativity of many of the Chinese art objects created after the end of the Cultural Revolution – but in our view also during the reign of Mao Zedong – is simply excellent. Modern Chinese art will not disappear in the future. However, we have the feeling that those works that will be appreciated in the long run are not necessarily identical with the works that are currently so trendy. The art works now in focus are only a small percentage of those worth collecting. This is a consequence of the current gold rush symptoms of the Chinese art market. But is it only a byproduct of Chinese economic progress and is this art worthless? Certainly, the present situation of the Chinese art market is a product of the Chinese empire-orientated policy. China is establishing itself as an empire, but not of any ordinary variety. The Chinese empire is an Empire of Globalization. It seeks not to conquer by the means of military superiority but rather to control by expanding its economy and culture. Controlled art might be profitable and useful, but it is impossible to control art for that would mean to control human minds. So far, the Chinese policy was very successful, but there might come a time in a not so distant future when the art will prove itself to be a key element in changing the face of China.

[22] Wu Hung, *Exhibiting Experimental Art in China*, Chicago: University of Chicago Press, 2006.

Bibliography

Andrews Julia F. and Shen Kuiyi, *A Century in Crisis: Modernity and Tradition in the Art of Twentieth-Century China*, New York: Guggenheim Museum, 1998.

„Art," *Britannica Encyclopedia internet edition,* http://www.britannica.com/EBchecked/topic/630806/art/ (February 2, 2012).

Barboza David, "Booming Chinese Art Market – Report," *The New York Times*, January 4, 2007.

Barboza David, "Some Contemporary Chinese Artists Are Angry About an April Auction at Sotheby's," *The New York Times*, May 7, 2008.

Croizier Ralph, *When Was Modern Chinese art? A short history of Chinese modernism*, in: *Writing Modern Chinese Art: Historiographic Explorations*, ed. by Josh Yiu, Seattle: Seattle Art Museum and University of Washington Press, 2009.

"Form 10-Q for SOTHEBYS," *Quarterly Report*, November 9, 2011, http://biz.yahoo.com/e/111109/bid10-q.html (February 2, 2012).

"Going, going, up. Easy money is pouring into the modern-art world," *The Economist*, January 11, 2007, http://www.economist.com/node/8522411 (February 2, 2012).

Chiu Melissa, *Chinese Contemporary Art: 7 Things You Should Know*, New York: AW Asia, 2008.

Chow Tse-Tsung, *The May Fourth Movement. Intellectual Revolution in Modern China*, Cambridge/Massachusetts: Harvard University (Harvard East Asian Studies, 6.), xvii, 1960.

Dangdai Yishu Huigui Xueshu Yishu Shi Cheng "Jingji Zhibiao" Jichu, January 6, 2011, http://arts.cul.sohu.com/20110106/n278707426.shtml (February 2, 2012).

Gao Mobo, *The Battle for China's Past: Mao and the Cultural Revolution*, London: Pluto Press, 2008.

Law Kam-yee, *The Chinese Cultural Revolution Reconsidered: beyond purge and Holocaust*, New York: Palgrave Macmillan 2003.

Li Zehou, *The Chinese aesthetic tradition*, Honolulu: University of Hawaii Press, 2010.

Meurer Cathryn, "Move over Mao: Do China's artists serve a new master?," *CNN*, http://www.cnn.com/SPECIALS/1999/china.50/inside.china/art.overview/ (February 2, 2012).

Pomfret James, "Chinese art sales weak in Sotheby's HK auction," *Reuters*, October 8, 2008, http://www.reuters.com/article/2008/10/08/us-art-china-sothebys-idUSTRE4972LU20081008 (February 2, 2012).

Wanczura Dieter, "Booming Chinese Art Market," *Artelino*, February 2007, http://www.artelino.com/articles/booming-chinese-art-market.asp (February 2, 2012).

Wanczura Dieter, "CNN on the Chinese Market of Contemporary Art," *Artelino*, February 2007, http://www.artelino.com/articles/booming-chinese-art-market.asp (February 2, 2012).

Wollheim Richard, *Art and its Objects*, Cambridge: Cambridge University Press, 1980.

Wu Hung, *Exhibiting Experimental Art in China*, Chicago: University of Chicago Press, 2006.

Zhang Xudong, *On Some Motifs in the Chinese "Cultural Fever" of the Late 1980s, Social Change, Ideology and Theory*, No. 39, Summer, 1994, Duke University Press.

Chapter Four

Janusz Bąbel

The Modernization of the People's Liberation Army since 1978

Key factors in the army modernization process

In the early 21st century, China is considered to be one of the world powers. In the field of economics such statement seems to be scientifically confirmed, particularly by China's third place in the world as regards GDP.[1] However, in relation to the Chinese military power it may seem questionable. On one hand, it should be stressed that the People's Republic of China has the largest army in the world, and is also one of the nuclear powers. What is worth mentioning is that during the last decade, China was actively involved in peacekeeping operations around the world. On the other hand, it should be noted that its technical advancements and equipment, despite the improvement in the last few decades, still does not allow to recognize the Chinese armed forces as capable of operating in the same conditions as other great powers in the Asia-Pacific region.

In the beginning, the process of PLA's modernization was as part of a broader program called the Four Modernizations. The process was initiated by Deng Xiaoping during the Third Plenum of the 11th Central Committee in December 1978. This process and its impact on PRC's military potential are the main subjects of this paper. The main theses of modernization were drawn by Zhou Enlai, and they included the following areas: agriculture, industry, trade, and military issues. In 1976, shortly after the death of Mao Zedong, the struggle for power between three major groups in the Chinese Communist Party (CCP) began. These were:

[1] *China. The World Factbook*, https://www.cia.gov/library/publications/the-world-factbook/geos/ch.html (April 25, 2010).

reformers, concentrated around Deng Xiaoping, CCP's ultra-leftist faction known as the Gang of Four, and Hua Guofeng's group. Hua Guofeng was designated by Mao as his successor. In this factional dispute, the PLA supported, though not unanimously, the reformist group. The reason for this behavior was the desire to take revenge for the purge of the military during the Cultural Revolution conducted by the people connected with the Gang of Four. However, the PLA was lacking full confidence in the reformers. At a critical time, support for this project was given by Hua Guofeng who was afraid of Jiang Qing's position. With the support of Marshal Ye Jianying and Wang Dongxiang, commander of Unit 8341 whose duty was to secure the safety of the PRC's leaders, a coup took place. On the night of 5th/6th October 1976, the Gang of Four was removed from power.[2]

In exchange for support the PLA forced the party leaders to agree on the return of Deng Xiaoping who was connected with the activists in the army and enjoyed the strong support among them from the beginning. Over the next two years, Hua Guofeng, although had at least titular power concentrated in his hands, was not sure of his position. The 11th Party Congress held in August 1977 confirmed only that the party was still divided. In this situation, due to swelling economic problems (decrease in agricultural and industrial production), social unrest, and changes in the international arena the next phase of the struggle for power within the CCP began. The third plenum of the Central Committee proved to be decisive. During the plenum, the program of the Four Modernization, strongly advocated by Deng, was initiated. It was a defeat for Hua Guofeng. Over the next three years he was slowly losing his position and influence in the party. In 1981, he gave up the party leadership to Hu Yaobang, and the leadership of the Central Military Commission was passed into the hands of Deng Xiaoping. Since this moment, the reformers concentrated the power and their activity on the modernization process, with the support of Prime Minister Zhao Ziyang who took over the seat in September 1980. Those events gave them a free hand in implementing the reforms that were already announced.[3]

The process of reforms in the PLA was speeded up by certain events. Such events can be divided into two subgroups, which will undergo a more detailed analysis. The first group is formed in the international events. The second group consists of some China's internal issues.

The first of these factors accelerating the modernization of the PLA was the unification of Vietnam in 1976. The Vietnamese state was for many years supported by the PRC in the struggle against the USA. In the

[2] Jakub Polit, *Chiny*, Warszawa: Wydawnictwo Trio, 2004, p. 270.

[3] *Ibid.*, p. 277–278.

end, it became a close ally of the Soviet Union, with whom the PRC competed for leadership in the communist block. In 1978, Vietnamese troops invaded Cambodia, ruled by the Khmer Rouge, and put an end to the criminal system created by Pol Pot. In the same year, Vietnam joined The Council for Mutual Economic Assistance, and signed an alliance treaty with the USSR. Beijing could no longer look at the growing potential threat at its southern border. Vietnam had already expanded its sphere of influence in Laos, making this country its puppet. Therefore, almost the entire Indochina was in the hands of Hanoi. The reason for the war was the issue of Chinese minority, who were persecuted by the Vietnamese authorities, and the territorial dispute concerning the Spratly Islands occupied by Vietnam.

Deng Xiaoping perfectly understood that in order to modernize the army that so far had been trained for the Maoist People's War model to a fully modern armed forces he would have to first overcome resistance within the party. He needed to convince the CCP that the reform of military bodies was crucial. To obtain evidence and to rely on the theorem proposed by the reformers to "seek truth from facts" he decided to invade the southern neighbor of the PRC. The operation was launched on 17th February, and lasted until 16th March 1979. Armed with obsolete equipment, poorly led, and trained army was unable to defeat the enemy hardened by almost 30 years of fighting. Vietnamese troops were not destroyed, and preserved their fighting ability, effectively dodging blows from the PLA, and using guerrilla warfare tactics perfectly mastered over several decades. It was a shame for the Chinese army, but Beijing considered the whole operation as a political success.

This war was the proof that Deng was waiting for to convince the undecided about the necessity to introduce changes. High losses in men and equipment, which compared to the modern Vietnamese gear (supplied by both the Soviets and the U.S. captured equipment), proved that the army was not fit for modern battlefield. The lack of adequate means of communication, and the obsolete doctrine of the People's War led to a military defeat. Losses on the side of China amounted to 25,000 killed and 37,000 wounded.[4]

For Vietnam it was also not an expected victory. Although it defended its independence, it suffered huge losses in the infrastructure which resulted from the fact that the Chinese troops occupied the northern part of the country. The Vietnamese government was also convinced that the treaty of alliance which bound it with the USSR did not oblige Moscow to any help. The lack of further progress of the Chinese troops to the south

[4] Zhang Xiaoming, "China's 1979 War with Vietnam: A Reassessment," *China Quarterly*, No. 184, Cambridge University Press, December 2005, p. 851–874.

resulted only from the absence of decision on the Chinese side about the need for further fighting.[5]

The described intervention snatched Vietnam from the Soviet sphere of influence and strengthened the unofficial Chinese alliance with the United States which may be counted on the account of Beijing as a success. However, border clashes between the two countries lasted until 1989, when Vietnam withdrew its forces from Cambodia, and China was in an awkward position due to the Tiananmen Square massacre. Border agreement with the re-demarcation of the border was signed in 1999.[6] This, however did not end the conflict between the two countries. Paracel and Spratly Islands remain a disputable area, since both parties, as well as other countries, usurp their rights to them.[7]

The year 1979 also brought another event on the international arena, from which the Chinese military theorists have drawn serious conclusions. On 26th December 1979, the Soviet invasion of Afghanistan began. China did not participate in the war that took nearly ten years, however PRC was one of the countries supporting the *mujaheddin*. It was an extremely difficult terrain where the partisans conducted guerrilla actions conventional methods of warfare used by the Red Army were ineffective. The war in Afghanistan is considered the beginning of the so-called Revolution in military affairs (RMA acronym comes from the English Revolution in Military Affairs).[8]

The most important conflict of the abovementioned revolution is the First Gulf War. Immediate intervention of the Allied Forces in 1991 showed the importance of information, modern communication, the doctrine of combined arms, and aviation support for the modern battlefield.[9] American intervention was used as a base for research for the PLA, supplemented with in-depth analysis of fighting in the valley of Becca and the Falklands War. The theory, however, was put into practice by the Chinese armed forces in 1995–1996, during the so-called Third Taiwanese Crisis. The PLA conducted extensive missile tests in the Taiwan strait. The Chinese armed forces, however, showed no significant changes nei-

[5] Polit, *op. cit.*, p. 280; Xinhui, *The Political History of Sino-Vietnamese War of 1979, and the Chinese Concept of Active Defense*, http://www.china-defense.com/history/sino-vn_1/sino-vn_1-1.html (April 25, 2010).

[6] Owen Bennett-Jones, "China-Vietnam pact signed," *BBC*, December 25, 2000, http://news.bbc.co.uk/2/hi/asia-pacific/1086867.stm available (April 25, 2010).

[7] *Konflikty współczesnego świata*, Warszawa: Wydawnictwo Naukowe PWN, 2008, p. 127–128.

[8] Marek Borucki, *Historia powszechna 1945–1999*, Warszawa: Wydawnictwo MADA, 2000, p. 183–186.

[9] Charles F. Hawkins, "The People's Liberation Army Looks to the Future," *Joint Force Quarterly*, Washington: National Defense University Press, Summer 2000, p. 12–16.

ther in the doctrine nor in equipment. These actions had an adverse effect on China, i.e. USS Nimitz battlegroup arrived at the Taiwan Strait . It was the first U.S. deployment in this region since 1976.[10]

In the last decade of the 20th century, there was also a serious discord between the PRC and the USA. On 6th April 1999 during the bombing of Belgrade, U.S. planes fired three missiles that hit the Chinese embassy. As a result, three people were killed and twenty were wounded. According to some sources the attack was deliberate, and was associated with an attempt to prevent the Chinese from obtaining the F-117 USAF wreck that was shot down over Serbia few days earlier. It is suspected that the analysis of the wreck was conducted by the Chinese intelligence services.[11] Recent conflicts in the world were also carefully observed by the PRC. Chinese military theorists were trying to draw conclusions, and accelerate the modernization of the PRC's armed forces by learning their lessons from the United States's response to the attack on the World Trade Center on 11th September 2001. The global war on terror and the involvement of coalition forces in the invasion of Afghanistan, and then Iraq confirmed the articled thesis of the leaders of the PRC. The U.S. are still technologically and organizationally superior to any other military power in the world. On the other hand, the involvement of armed forces in counter-terrorism specific to asymmetric warfare necessitate a redefinition of military doctrines. The increasing threat of terrorism and maritime piracy has prompted the authorities in Beijing to engage the armed forces in peacekeeping, stabilization, and maritime patrols to protect shipping lines necessary for the maintenance of China's economic growth.

The second group of events accelerating the modernization are the events that took place in China. The 1980s brought changes in the economy which was freed from the rigid central planning economy characteristic of the previous period. The first changes were associated with the creation of special economic zones – specific windows to the world. Along with the opening to China, Western values slowly entered the country.

After the change in control that took place in 1976–1981, the army lost some of its influence on domestic policy which it had since the Cultural Revolution, when it was actually the PLA's vanguard. An additional argument lowering the enthusiasm towards economic reform was the fact that the army was no longer the only path to guarantee successful career both in social and economic sphere. The military was most severely influenced by reduced funding, which constituted to almost 5 percent of

[10] *Ibid.*, p. 13.

[11] "Atak na ambasadę Chin w Belgradzie", in: Piotr Bein, *NATO na Bałkanach*, March 24, 2000, http://www.gavagai.pl/nato/ambasada.htm (April 25, 2010).

GDP at the beginning of the modernization process, and then dropped to 1 percent, while funding for other departments was increased. It was a signal that the Fourth Modernization was not a priority for the CCP.[12]

Deng understood the need to reduce expenditure on the army in order to accelerate the reforms, which is why the Sino-Vietnamese war was for him a great excuse to make cuts. In the 1970s, PLA remained Mao Zedong's political tool. As regards politics the army was shaped during the office of Lin Biao, Mao Zedong's close collaborator. The famous *Little Red Book* was then compiled as a manual for the army.[13] In 1984, the restoration of the ranks in the PLA took place. Reduction in size of the army contributed to the improvement of its quality. The reduction influenced mostly support formations, and in the officer corps – supporters of people's war and Deng Xiaoping's opponents.[14]

However, the purchase of newest technology weapons, which were supposed to improve the army's efficiency, was interrupted in 1989. The events in the Tiananmen Square threw a long shadow on the PLA. Again, the army was used as a tool of domestic politics, for the majority of the army became merely the guardian of the regime or a fright for the competing factions within the CCP. The massacre in the square resulted in wide repercussions in the international arena. The United States and the countries of the European Communities condemned the Chinese government's solution to social unrest, and also imposed an embargo on the purchase of weapons. However, the repercussions did not last long due to the geopolitical changes in the Soviet bloc and the Middle East. Officially, the embargo remains in force until today, but China procures weapons both in Europe and the United States from civilian sources or through unofficial channels.[15]

The slow process of transferring power began also in China. Deng Xiaoping anointed his successor – Jiang Zemin. This civilian official, the mayor of Shanghai, took over Deng's chair in the Central Military Commission in November 1989. It was not by an accident, since that body began the transfer of leadership. Deng understood that after the events of June 1989, he could secure a peaceful transition of power into the hands of a successor only with the support of the army. Jiang Zemin, who had held the highest offices in the party and the state for over a decade, effectively took advantage of the support of the army at that time. An opportunity came in 1992, when Yang Baibing and Yang Shangkun tried to

[12] John Gittings, *Historia współczesnych Chin*, Kraków: Wydawnictwo Uniwersytetu Jagiellońskiego, 2010, p. 191–192.

[13] *Ibid.*, p. 191.

[14] Polit, *op. cit.*, p. 302.

[15] *Ibid.*, p. 314.

create a competition to Jiang's faction in the party as well in the military. As a result, they were removed from the Politburo Standing Committee by Deng Xiaoping. In their place technocrats – Zhu Rongji and Hu Jintao – were appointed. In 1998, limitation for production and service enterprises of the People's Liberation Army was enforced.[16] One can say that from that moment the party, and in fact the PRC's Central Military Commission, regained the overall impact on military operations.

The 1990s brought improvement in relations between the Russian Federation and China. As a result of the international situation, the PRC was forced to procure military equipment from Russia (incidentally, Israel was and still remains the second source). At the turn of the century, the supply of equipment covered warships, combat aircraft (e.g. Su-27), and electronic equipment.[17]

The next leader of the People's Republic of China, Hu Jintao, continued his predecessor's policies. It is worth noting that Hu Jintao previously was the Chairman of the PRC (15th March 2003) rather than the President of the Central Military Commission (19th September 2004). This allows to draw several conclusions. Jiang Zemin still retains a fairly large influence on both the structure of the party and the military. What is more, the military has an impact on the policy implemented by the CCP at all times.

Military financing

Since 1978, when the PRC started a broad program of reforms, it also began to gradually reduce the share of GDP in financing the army. The army, trying to settle in at the new situation, started to run its own business, and it became one of the major players in the property market in China. However, in the 1990s, PLA's financial independence was limited due to corruption scandals and the introduction of limitations in the scope of conducting business. Nevertheless, the PRC's expenditure on arms, although still relatively small, when taken into account by the percentage of GDP is still the second largest expenditure in the world. Table 1 shows the dynamics of the PRC's military spending in the years 1978–2007.

[16] Dongmin Lee, *Chinese Civil-Military Relations The Divestiture of People's Liberation Army Business Holdings*, http://afs.sagepub.com/content/32/3/437.abstract (April 25, 2010).

[17] Gittings, *op. cit.*, p. 309.

Table 1. PRC's military expenditure (1978–2007)

Year	GDP (in billion RMB)	GDP on military (in billion RMB)	Percent share of GDP on military matters
1978	364,522	16,784	4.6
1979	406,258	22,264	5.48
1980	454,562	19,384	4.26
1981	489,156	16,797	3.43
1982	532,335	17,635	3.31
1983	596,265	17,713	2.97
1984	720,805	18,076	2.51
1985	901,604	19,153	2.12
1986	1,027,518	20,075	1.95
1987	1,205,862	20,962	1.74
1988	1,504,282	21,800	1.45
1989	1,699,232	25,147	1.48
1990	1,866,782	29,031	1.56
1991	2,178,150	33,031	1.52
1992	2,692,348	37,786	1.40
1993	3,533,392	42,580	1.21
1994	4,819,786	55,071	1.14
1995	6,079,373	63,672	1.05
1996	7,117,659	72,006	1.01
1997	7,897,303	81,257	1.03
1998	8,440,228	93,470	1.11
1999	8,967,705	107,640	1.20
2000	9,921,455	120,754	1.22
2001	10,965,517	144,204	1.32
2002	12,033,269	170,778	1.42
2003	13,582,276	190,787	1.40
2004	15,987,834	220,001	1.38
2005	18,321,745	247,496	1.35
2006	21,192,346	297,938	1.41
2007	25,730,556	355,491	1.38

Source: *White paper on national defense*, Appendix V Defense Expenditure of the PRC (1978–2007), http://www.china.org.cn/government/whitepaper/2009-01/21/content_17162747.htm (April 25, 2010).

Today the PLA is aiming at smaller numbers but a more effective fighting force. Chinese military decline can be explained by several factors. First, the doctrine of popular war with massive attacks begins to be discarded. The second is connected with changes in financing of the army, reduction of its size and organizational changes. The decline is best illustrated by the following table.

Table 2. Quantity of the PLA's forces (1985–2005)

Year	Number of soldiers (in millions)
1985	4,238
1987	3,235
1990	3,199
2005 and following	2.3

Source: *PLA History*, http://www.globalsecurity.org/military/world/china/pla-history.htm (April 25, 2010).

These numbers include all of the Chinese armed forces organized into three main parts. The basic and most numerous are the Chinese Army's Land Forces. These include about 1.6 million soldiers grouped in about 70 mobile warfare compounds (including units from regiment to division level).In addition, there are 600 thousand military police officers and 800 thousand reserves. Therefore, all the groups amount to 3 million people in total.[18] These forces are grouped into 18 Army Groups. The PRC's Central Military Commission with its Chief, President Hu Jintao, supervised the whole structure. Apart from the enormous human reserves the PLA also had a huge reserve of hardware. Although most army equipment used by the Chinese was designed back in the 1950s and 1960s, its number still can be impressive, and discourage the enemies of China to take offensive action against the country.

The second part of the Chinese army is the PLA's Air Force. Their size is estimated at 400,000 troops, and the number of aircraft at nearly 2,000 machines. The tasks of this military aircraft is to protect the area belonging to the PRC. Another task of the Air Force is the nuclear deterrence, since the Air Force's strategic bombers have nuclear weapons carriers. Thus, apart from the military factor, the Air Force can be considered as

[18] *Ground Forces*, http://www.sinodefence.com/army/default.asp (April 25, 2010).

a psychological factor deterring the potential aggressor. The air units numbers also vary, depending on sources, from 1510[19] to 2000 aircrafts.[20]

The third type of the Chinese armed forces is the Navy. During the Cold War, the Chinese fleet was responsible only for the defense of China against amphibious landings which could be expected in the narrow, but very long, coast. Since the beginning of the 1990s, China began to develop a modern naval force capable of fighting not only in the coastal environment, but also able to 'project power' far beyond the coastal sea. It was a signal that China abandoned the so-called doctrine of brown water to blue water doctrine. The force of the Navy is estimated at nearly 250,000 soldiers and nearly 630 units.

In 1955, the PRC began a nuclear program. On 16th October 1964 the first successful nuclear attempt was held in the desert Lob Nor. Three years later, on 17th June 1967, China carried out the first hydrogen bomb test, thus entering the small club of nuclear superpowers.[21] It was achieved despite the breaking of the military-scientific cooperation between the USSR and the PRC. The number of warheads, depending on the sources, is estimated at from 150 to 400 warheads.[22] Nuclear forces are organized into the 2nd Artillery Corps and are strictly defensive. There are several reasons for this state of China's deterrent forces. Firstly, although the Middle Kingdom has been developing missile technology for nearly six decades, the Chinese rocket launchers, both land and submarine, reached the expected level of technology. Secondly, the problem of the lack of air carriers of a classical nuclear triad is still present. Chinese H-5 bombers (IL-28), capable of carrying tactical nuclear bombs, and H-6 (Tu-16 Badger) are strategic bombers of the Soviet production dating from 1950.[23] In the early 21st century, China begins the design modern vector of the nuclear triad. The DF-31 missiles and JIN class SSBN constitute the Chinese nuclear dyad. PLA is spending substantial part of its expenditure on modern intercontinental strategic bombers and missiles capable of carrying multiple warheads simultaneously.

[19] "World Military Aircraft Inventory," *Aviation Week & Space Technology. Source Book 2009*, http://www.aviationweek.com/awin/sourcebook/content.jsp?channelName=pro&story=xml/sourcebook_xml/2009/01/26/AW_01_26_2009_p0240-112924-32.xml&headline=World Military Aircraft Inventory – China (February 25, 2012).

[20] *Air Forces*, http://www.sinodefence.com/airforce/default.asp (April 25, 2010).

[21] *China's Nuclear Chronology*, The Nuclear Threat Initiative (NTI), http://www.nti.org/media/pdfs/china_nuclear.pdf?_=1316466791 (February 2, 2012).

[22] *Second Artillery Corps, Weapons of Mass Destruction (WMD)*, http://www.globalsecurity.org/wmd/world/china/2-corps.htm (April 25, 2010).

[23] Bill Gunston, *Ilustrowany przewodnik po nowoczesnych bombowcach*, Warszawa: Wydawnictwo Bellona, 2000, p. 82–85.

Currently, the strategy and doctrine of the PLA is the active defense strategy based on the people's war, and thus the concept derived from Mao Zedong.[24] In 2009, Hu Jintao redefined the role of the PLA in the Chinese defense policy; it is to guard:

- The CCP's status as the ruling power in China,
- Sovereignty,
- Territorial integrity,
- Internal security,
- The interests of the PRC,
- World peace.[25]

The leading think tanks analyzed the PLA's military experience of the last two decades trying to determine the future path of the Chinese armed forces. It is worth mentioning that the four main doctrines competed with one other. The first of these was the people's war version of active defense, which was outlined by Mao Zedong. This doctrine is still present and repeatedly expressed by the leaders of the PRC. However, it seems that it is so only in the ideological sphere. It should be stressed that maintaining this fiction does not interfere with the modernization of the army itself. The second doctrine was the doctrine of power projection promoted by neo-traditionalists. It assumes the creation of forces capable to carry the power out, not only in the close neighborhood, but also in other places in the world. Today, we can already see the elements in the activities of the PLA in the international arena. Among them one should mention the most tangible sign, i.e. is the participation of Chinese warships in anti-piracy patrols in the waters of the Indian Ocean, and the introduction of nuclear warships with nuclear warheads likely to hit targets in European countries or the United States.The third doctrine was introduced by Jiang Zemin in 1993. It was a revolution in military affairs (English acronym – RMA). It assumes the creation and use of technological superiority in the modern battlefield. RMA incorporated PRC's official defense policy to allocate a large part of research and development in order to reduce the technological gap separating China and Western countries. The result is the Chinese space program and a wide range of military capabilities in the field of activity in cyber war. The fourth doctrine, which has left its mark on the current PRC's defense doctrine, is the doctrine of unlimited war. Its proponents believe that the achievements of the RMA can be used in any way possible, such as hackers' attacks on

[24] See: Lt. Gen. Li Jijun, *Traditional Military Thinking and the Defensive Strategy of China*, Carlisle: U.S. Army War College, Strategic Studies Institute, 1997.

[25] Cortez A. Cooper, *The PLA Navy's "New Historic Missions": Expanding Capabilities for a Re-emergent Maritime Power*, RAND, June 11, 2009, http://www.rand.org/pubs/testimonies/2009/RAND_CT332.pdf (April 25, 2010).

public and financial institutions. There is also a view that this form of 'power projection' is only done by any available means, unless the totality of the action taken is a popular war in a new edition. All of the above doctrines were gradually incorporated into the strategy of the PRC because, as Charles Hawkins pointed out rightly, only compromise in the coexistence of these doctrines within the PLA can create modern armed forces that are able to achieve their tasks.[26]

Conclusions

The Chinese armed forces, despite all power and huge human resources potential to mobilize the army, are not ideal. Problems encountered by the PLA can be divided into several ranges that should be analyzed separately. At the technological level the PLA is still based on hardware equipment of Soviet or Russian origin introduced into the production 40 to 60 years ago. Examples of such equipment may be the units running D-20 armed with artillery, which were put into service in the 1940s, and type 59/69 tanks based on the Soviet T-55.[27] It is the way chosen by the Chinese leaders aimed at saving time and resources in the struggle to equip individuals in high-quality domestically produced equipment, e.g. armored forces of the PLA, which gradually introduce the latest generation of tanks Type 99. The Chinese air forces have also started to modernize their equipment. Aircrafts such as J-2, J-5, J-6, J-7 II are already outdated. With the help of the Russian Federation, close cooperation with Israel and Pakistan, as well as industrial espionage, China significantly increased their level of technical advancement in the field of aviation. Introduction of J-11 plane , entirely manufactured in the PRC, whose construction was based on Russian Su-27 and J-10, was to strengthen both offensive and defensive abilities of Chinese air forces.

The Chinese Navy is the most evident symbol of the new position of Chinese armed forces on the planet. New projects of Chinese warships – Jin SSBN Type 094, Type 051C Luzhou DDG, DDG Type 052C Luyang II, Type II FFG Jiangwei 057, allow the PRC to 'project its power' a global scale. Modern Chinese ships will successively replace those produced in the Soviet Union.

[26] Hawkins, *The Four Futures, Competing Schools of Military Thought inside the PLA*, March 2000, http://taiwansecurity.org/IS/IS-0300-Hawkins.htm (April 25, 2010).

[27] *People's Liberation Army – Ground, Army Equipment*, http://www.globalsecurity.org/military/world/china/pla-inventory.htm (April 25, 2010).

Bibliography

"Atak na ambasadę Chin w Belgradzie," in: Piotr Bein, *NATO na Bałkanach*, March 24, 2000, http://www.gavagai.pl/nato/ambasada.htm (April 25, 2010).

Air Forces, http://www.sinodefence.com/airforce/default.asp (April 25, 2010).

Bennett-Jones Owen, "China-Vietnam Pact Signed," *BBC*, December 25, 2000, http://news.bbc.co.uk/2/hi/asia-pacific/1086867.stm available (April 25, 2010).

Borucki Marek, *Historia powszechna 1945–1999*, Warszawa: Wydawnictwo MADA, 2000.

China. The World Factbook, https://www.cia.gov/library/publications/the-worldfactbook/geos/ch.html (April 25, 2010).

China's Nuclear Chronology, The Nuclear Threat Initiative (NTI), http://www.nti.org/media/pdfs/china_nuclear.pdf?_=1316466791 (February 2, 2012).

Cooper Cortez A., *The PLA Navy's "New Historic Missions:" Expanding Capabilities for a Re-emergent Maritime Power*, RAND, June 11, 2009, http://www.rand.org/pubs/testimonies/2009/RAND_CT332.pdf (April 25, 2010).

Gittings John, *Historia współczesnych Chin*, Kraków: Wydawnictwo Uniwersytetu Jagiellońskiego, 2010.

Ground Forces, http://www.sinodefence.com/army/default.asp (April 25, 2010).

Gunston Bill, *Ilustrowany przewodnik po nowoczesnych bombowcach*, Warszawa: Wydawnictwo Bellona, 2000.

Hawkins Charles F., "The People's Liberation Army Looks to the Future," *Joint Force Quarterly*, Washington: National Defense University Press, Summer 2000.

Hawkins Charles F., *The Four Futures, Competing Schools of Military Thought inside the PLA*, March 2000, http://taiwansecurity.org/IS/IS-0300-Hawkins.htm (April 25, 2010).

Konflikty współczesnego świata, Warszawa: Wydawnictwo PWN, 2008.

Lee Dongmin, *Chinese Civil-Military Relations The Divestiture of People's Liberation Army Business Holdings*, http://afs.sagepub.com/content/32/3/437.abstract (April 25, 2010).

Li Jijun, *Traditional Military Thinking and the Defensive Strategy of China*, Carlisle: U.S. Army War College, Strategic Studies Institute, 1997.

People's Liberation Army – Ground, Army Equipment, http://www.globalsecurity.org/military/world/china/pla-inventory.htm (April 25, 2010).

PLA History, http://www.globalsecurity.org/military/world/china/pla-history.htm (April 25, 2010).

Polit Jakub, *Chiny*, Warszawa: Wydawnictwo Trio, 2004.

Second Artillery Corps, Weapons of Mass Destruction (WMD), http://www.globalsecurity.org/wmd/world/china/2-corps.htm (April 25, 2010).

White paper on national defense, Appendix V Defense Expenditure of the PRC (1978–2007), http://www.china.org.cn/government/whitepaper/2009-01/21/content_17162747.htm (April 25, 2010).

"World Military Aircraft Inventory," *Aviation Week & Space Technology. Source Book 2009*, http://www.aviationweek.com/awin/sourcebook/content.jsp?channelName=pro&story=xml/sourcebook_xml/2009/01/26/AW_01_26_2009_p0240-112924-32.xml&headline=World Military Aircraft Inventory_China (February 25, 2012).

Xinhui, *The Political History of Sino-Vietnamese War of 1979, and the Chinese Concept of Active Defense*, http://www.china-defense.com/history/sino-vn_1/sino-vn_1-1.html (April 25, 2010).

Zhang Xiaoming, "China's 1979 War with Vietnam: A Reassessment," *China Quarterly*, No. 184, Cambridge University Press, December 2005.

Chapter Five

Paweł Bieńkowski

The Reduced Role of the People's Liberation Army in the Political Succession to Deng Xiaoping and to Jiang Zemin: Chinese Style Civilian-Military Relations in the Making

When Jiang Zemin rose to power as Deng Xiaoping's successor in 1989 without any major obstacles from the People's Liberation Army's leadership, it became evident how enormous evolution has the Chinese military undergone. From the Maoist "party-army" of the Long March and the beginning of the People's Republic of China (PRC), it was transformed into an ever-modernising force with its relations with the state organisation more likely to be characterised as resembling "civil-military."[1] This trend was even reinforced by Hu Jintao's succession in 2002, again under similar circumstances. Truly, the nowadays People's Liberation Army (PLA) plays a significantly less important role in Chinese public affairs than it used to play before. This includes the army's engagement in the issues of political ascendancy and the switch in power. The paper aims at giving some reasons for a limited influence of the army on the succession to both Deng Xiaoping and Jiang Zemin, with an insight into a matter of today's links between the army, the Party and the Chinese state. It traces the evolution of PLA's status in Chinese internal politics from the time of Mao, until the present day, and describes some basic features of the current model of "civil-military relations with Chinese characteristics".

[1] David Shambaugh, "Civil-Military Relations in China: Party-Army or National Military?," *Copenhagen Journal of Asian Studies*, Vol. 16, 2002, p. 11.

Maoist legacy and Dengist reform

As mentioned above, the military involvement in Chinese politics has a rich tradition. Even though party-army relations have always been characterised by the classic Mao's wisdom that "political power grows out of the barrel of the gun. (...) The party must always control the gun, the gun must never control the party," the PLA's role in public matters in some periods was deeply appreciated.[2] Both Mao and Deng could use the military force in critical moments in order to strengthen their position with almost undisputable certainty of the military leaders' compliance.[3] Consequently, the military was always subject to the absolute sovereignty of the Chinese Communist Party (CCP) under the Maoist model of the "party-army." Under such a guidance, the military was supposed to be "a tool used in order to achieve certain political objectives." Its features included, inter alia, promoting soldiers' political indoctrination over their combat readiness, maintaining strict connections between the army and society, adopting the strategy of "People's War," introducing some sort of "intra-army democracy", obliging the military to fulfill certain economic duties in favour of the people, treating the army as "an example" for the society, and, what is crucial, maintaining no distinct division between civilian and military leadership.[4] Largely, the PLA was manoeuvred into the internal political conflict, and became the basis of Mao's revolutionary strategy. Despite the fact that the military circles had dared to express their dissatisfaction with entering the Korean war in 1950, despite the criticism of the Great Leap Forward by Marshal Peng Dehuai, and an unusual growth in the power of Marshal Lin Biao, the Party managed to control the military continuously and to prevent the PLA from intervening into politics on its own.[5]

The policies of Mao's successor, Deng Xiaoping, resulted in necessary modernisations and a long-desired internal order.[6] Traditionally, according to Harry Harding, the PLA used to be more active when both the Party and the state were weaker, and, respectively, more autonomous when these two structures appeared to be stronger.[7] As soon as the latter situa-

[2] June Teufel Dreyer, *China's Political System: Modernization and Tradition*, New York: Pearson Education, 2008, p. 191.

[3] Ellis Joffe, *The Chinese Army in Domestic Politics. Factors and Phases*, in: *Chinese Civil--Military Relations. The Transformation of the People's Liberation Army*, ed. by Nan Li, London: Routledge, 2006, p. 13–15.

[4] Dreyer, *op. cit.*, p. 191.

[5] *Ibid.*, p. 196–200; *Chinese Civil-Military Relations..., op. cit.*, p. 10; James C.F. Wang, *Contemporary Chinese Politics: An Introduction*, New York: Prentice Hall, Upper Saddle River, 2002, p. 241.

[6] Joffe, *op. cit.*, p. 12.

[7] Harry Harding, *The Role of the Military in Chinese Politics*, in: *Citizens and Groups in*

tion prevailed, the army had no choice but to retreat to its original role of the country's defender. The generals' confidence was obviously reinforced by the knowledge of military affairs the war-experienced Deng Xiaoping had. However, his "Four Modernisations" eventually put the reforms of the army on the last place, while the leader himself suggested the generals to seek economic self-reliance, which eventually gave rise to a unique business empire driven by soldiers, and known among the scholars as the "PLA Inc."[8] As a result, during the 1980s, PLA was diverted by two different activities: engagement in the already mentioned army-owned enterprises and the modernisation of armed forces.[9] The former resulted in an increase in internal funds of the military organisation, but also in such negative outcomes as corruption, decrease in soldiers' morale, and damage of the image of the army among the Chinese people.[10] The latter was, at the same time, a still developing process, motivated by an enormous technological gap between the PLA and other, especially Western, militaries. An insufficient progress of these efforts, caused, among other, by PLA's non-military internal involvement, resulted in a 'shock' the Chinese commanders suffered in 1991, as they observed the performance of the American-led coalition forces during the Gulf War.[11] The PLA, by that time having been made self-sufficient by Deng's policies, had to deal with many other peculiar problems, e.g. a decrease in recruits among the peasantry (caused by economic growth in agriculture, making this sector more profitable than military service) and a struggle with educating the officer corps.[12]

Another reason for the army's non-involvement in internal politics was its changing operational doctrine. In 1985, the Central Military Commission (CMC), the Chinese 'supreme command,' issued a new set of guidance, finally approving the most recent step in the evolution of the Chinese security concept. A Maoist doctrine of "People's War," although still serving as a foundation of the entire strategic thinking in the PRC, was eventually upgraded into an all-new concept of "local, limited war" along the country's borders, fought with a high-tech weaponry.[13] As the following years showed, this shift in the doctrine was of a profound sig-

Contemporary China, ed. by Victor C. Falkenheim, Ann Arbor: University of Michigan Center for Chinese Studies, 1987, p. 213–256.

[8] Thomas J. Bickford, *The People's Liberation Army and Its Changing Economic Roles. Implications for Civil-Military Relations*, in: *Chinese Civil-Military Relations...*, *op. cit.*, p. 161–162.

[9] Joffe, *op. cit.*, p. 12.

[10] Bickford, *op. cit.*, p. 166–168.

[11] Dreyer, *op. cit.*, p. 204.

[12] Wang, *op. cit.*, p. 249–251.

[13] Dennis J. Blasko, *The Chinese Army Today: Tradition and Transformation of the 21st* Century, Abingdon: Routledge, 2006, p. 5, 11–12.

nificance for the army's modernisation. The current "National Military Strategic Guidelines for the New Period," probably approved in 1993, re-adjusted Mao's concept of "active defence" and "non-war use of force," which assumed a quick and offensive reaction for a threat to national sovereignty and territorial integrity.[14] This doctrine requires a rapid development of poor Chinese capabilities of power-projection, and thus seems to pose a major task, attracting the attention of Chinese military leaders for a long time to come.

Additionally, the PLA might have been ousted from the succession to Deng Xiaoping because of a major internal restructuring of its leadership at the final stage of his rule. This refers to the changes that followed the Tiananmen incident, including a purge within the CMC and the PLA officer corps.[15] During the crisis, the army was expected to execute direct political orders; consequently, the officers, not eager to comply with the supreme command's directives, were removed or reshuffled.[16] The hard-liners, Yang Shangkun and his half-brother Yang Baibing, who briefly dominated the CMC, were eventually removed by Deng in 1992 with an approval from the PLA.[17] These actions have strengthened the position of the emerging new leader: Jiang Zemin. Being aware of the fact that the military leaders had opposed a perspective of Hu Yaobang becoming the supreme leader, Deng even held a personal meeting with high-ranked generals in March 1995 (with his health conditions deteriorating) in order to assure them regarding Jiang.[18]

Jiang and Hu: civilians taking over

Under such circumstances, Jiang Zemin assumed the top party and state positions in 1989 as the first supreme leader of the PRC deprived of any military credentials. In order to gain and solidify his power over the military, Jiang made a "bargain" with the military leaders: as long as the Party supports PLA's budget, the army does not question his leadership.[19] Additionally, Jiang has built his power over the army in a classic Chinese style:

[14] *Annual Report on Military Power of the People's Republic of China*, The US Secretary of Defense, 2008, p. 16–17.

[15] Wang, *op. cit.*, p. 243; Shambaugh, *Modernizing China's Military: Progress, Problems and Prospects*, Berkeley: University of California Press, 2002, p. 21.

[16] Wang, *op. cit.*, p. 244; Shambaugh, *Modernizing China's Military...*, p. 21.

[17] Ji You, *Sorting Out the Myths About Political Commissars*, in: *Chinese Civil-Military Relations...*, *op. cit.*, p. 114.

[18] Wang, *op. cit.*, p. 242, 255.

[19] Shambaugh, *Civil-Military Relations...*, *op. cit.*, p. 20.

deriving it from the overall power he possessed within the party and state structure.[20] This possibility to 'hire and fire' tends to be crucial in maintaining control over any organisation, military in particular. Jiang used it perfectly by retiring generals reluctant to him and promoting younger ones, who did not have any advantage of age over him.[21] Probably, the best proof of success of such policy was the strong support Jiang received from the generals both in 2002 and 2003, when he was still the chairman of CMC, even though Hu Jintao had already replaced him as the head of state.[22] However, during a series of crisis outbreaks regarding Taiwan between 1993 and 1996, the PLA establishment expressed its dissatisfaction with a line adopted by Jiang; the latter evidently tried to appease the military by giving the generals the right to participate in a key party body dealing with Taiwan affairs: Taiwan Affairs Leading Small Group.[23] All these actions have finally brought their anticipated objectives: Jiang's power over the military was big enough for him to order a long-desired divestiture of army enterprises in 1998, and to move a bargain of financing national defence expenditures from the military and party structures directly and officially to the state budget.[24]

Hu Jintao took over from Jiang in 2002, becoming the second leader without any military background. Circumstances surrounding his growth into power constitute a strong point justifying army's retreat from high-level internal politics, known as the breakdown of the so called 'interlocking directorate' in key party structures. Originally, under a Leninist model of party-army relations, military officers used to have a significant share in the membership of CCP's Central Committee and its Politburo, resulting in the PLA's influence on party and state politics. This influence was balanced by the existence of Party committees and cells within army units, and cultivation of the 'nomenclature' system tying together the issues of professional career with party membership and support.[25] However, due to the succession of a new generation of leaders (so called 'the fourth'), inexperienced in military affairs, this unique symbiosis of Party and army structures broke down: an amount of armed forces' representatives in the Central Committee has fallen to about 20 percent, without

[20] Joffe, *op. cit.*, p. 15.

[21] *Ibid.*, p. 16; Dreyer, *op. cit.*, p. 125.

[22] Joseph Fewsmith, *China Since Tiananmen: From Deng Xiaoping to Hu Jintao*, Cambridge: Cambridge University Press, 2008, p. 250, 254.

[23] *Chinese Civil-Military Relations..., op. cit.*, p. 16; Tai Ming Cheung, *The Influence of the Gun: China's CMC and Its Relationship with the Military, Party, and State Decision-Making Systems*, in: David M. Lampton, *The Making of Chinese Foreign and Security Policy in the Era of Reform*, Stanford: Stanford University Press, 2001, p. 67, 85.

[24] Bickford, *op. cit.*, p. 168.

[25] Shambaugh, *Civil-Military Relations...*, p. 13.

even a single left in the Standing Committee of the Politburo (after the Sixteenth Party Congress).[26] In 2002, only two PLA generals in the central command level possessed any satisfying experience in the supreme-level national politics.[27] Additionally, the issues of career opportunities and promotion were becoming more and more professionalised, with more and more officers being promoted to higher ranks thanks to their personal achievements rather than party background.[28] Under such circumstances, direct influence the army was able to exert on matters of political succession seemed to be faint. James Mulvenon predicts that this trend can even deepen with a succession of the non-technocratic 'fifth generation' of leadership, totally pulling out the remaining army technocrats.[29]

According to David Shambaugh, the 16th Party Congress of 2002 brought the most comprehensive 'turnover' of the Chinese military leadership in the history; and what is more, this change was carried out in an entirely peaceful way.[30] After the Congress, the CMC's size was reduced from 11 to 8 members, most of whom are now experienced army professionals who truly deserved their current positions due to their personal achievements.[31] Obviously, such a development can be regarded as a milestone in the professionalization of Chinese civil-military relations. What particularly matters to Hu Jintao's rise to power, is the fact that Jiang Zemin was reappointed the chairman of CMC. While Hu, similarly to Jiang, had not managed to gain the PLA's respect by the time he succeeded Jiang as the state and party chief, Jiang's decision to remain the PLA's commander-in-chief can be examined as a sort of 'favour' towards his political successor during this 'transitional period'. Eventually, after Hu had succeeded Jiang on the chair of CMC in 2004, there were no signs of the PLA's discontent.

---

[26] Shambaugh, *The Changing of the Guard: China's New Military Leadership*, in: Yun-han Chu, Chih-cheng Lo, and Ramon H. Myers, *The New Chinese Leadership: Challenges and Opportunities after the 16th Party Congress*, Cambridge: Cambridge University Press, 2004, p. 90–91.

[27] Shambaugh, *Civil-Military Relations...*, p. 12. These two generals were Chi Haotian and Wang Ruilin.

[28] *Ibid*, p. 13.

[29] James C. Mulvenon, *Straining Against the Yoke? Civil-Military Relations in China After the Seventeenth Party Congress*, in: *China's Changing Political Landscape: Prospects for Democracy*, ed. by Cheng Li, Washington: Brookings Institution Press, 2008, p. 89.

[30] Shambaugh, *The Changing of the Guard...*, p. 89.

[31] *Ibid.*, p. 90–96.

Legal, financial and institutional aspects

Legal documents adopted by PRC's key state organs also contain some crucial stipulations regarding the relationship between the Party, the state, and the military. However, before going into detail, one must acknowledge the provisions of the 1982 PRC constitution which subordinates the entire state structure to the CCP and underlines the party's leadership over the military. At the same time, current Chinese legal doctrine establishes the precedence of legislation in favour of the National People's Congress which is clearly a state body. This potential clash of authority can be explained in no other way than by the existence of a total control of state structures by the CCP. According to Jeremy Paltiel, PLA's political role defines the monopoly of the ruling CCP on power; this power is eventually maintained with the resort to military force.[32] One of the most crucial documents describing contemporary civil-military relations in China is the National Defence Law (NDL), adopted by the National People's Congress in 1997. This regulation provides general guidelines on functioning of the armed forces within the PRC, with a special emphasis on a *de facto* nominal subordination of the PLA to the state. In this context, according to NDL, PLA comes under scrutiny of various governmental bodies; terms of introducing the state of emergency and martial law are defined; responsibilities of the military towards the state are enumerated; the matters of leading the armed forces are presented. [33] To sum up, the rhetoric layer of the document suggests at least some shift towards more Huntingtonian, state-military relations in legal terms, but still under an overwhelming control of the dominant party. At the same time, with a division of power between CCP and the state structure just emerging, the army seems to be taking a neutral stand, counting on some likely benefits in the future.[34]

More specific, PLA-oriented documents seem to follow the established guidance. As far as the issue of supervision over the military is concerned, the *Military Service Law of the People's Republic of China* (adopted in 1984 and revised in 1998) in its Article 10 reads: "Responsibility for military service work throughout the country shall be assumed by the Ministry of National Defence under the leadership of the State Council and the Central Military Commission".[35]

---

[32] Jeremy T. Paltiel, "PLA Allegiance on Parade: Civil-Military Relations in Transition," *The China Quarterly*, Vol. 143, 1995, p. 786–787.

[33] Shambaugh, *Civil-Military Relations...*, p. 20–23.

[34] *Ibid.*, p. 26.

[35] *Military Service Law of the People's Republic of China*, Military Laws and Regulations, http://english.chinamil.com.cn/site2/special-reports/2006-04/20/content_460092.htm (February 2, 2012).

This regulation seems to name state institutions under the guidance of the CMC as watchdogs of PLA's activities. Similarly, according to the *Law of the People's Republic of China on Officers in Active Service* (adopted in 1988), "Officers constitute part of the State functionaries" (article 3).[36] However, recent amendments to this document (accepted in December 2000) require, inter alia, the PLA officers to be "(...) loyal to the motherland and to the Communist Party of China".[37] All things considered, these examples of Chinese military guidelines can suggest a slow and careful nominal shift of army's loyalty from the CCP to the state structure. Nonetheless, the nature of a one-party political system of today's PRC leaves no doubt on who really controls "the gun".

A question worth asking is the price the Party had to pay for the military to stay out of politics. Basically, after an unavoidable divestiture of PLA-held business holdings ordained in 1998, CCP was obliged to provide the army with higher budgetary funds in order to satisfy its enormous modernisation needs. Indeed, according to the SIPRI database, military expenditure in China rose by nearly 15 percent from year to year (1997 to 1998) following the dismantling of army enterprises. This particular growth, initiated even one year earlier, could be interpreted as a sort of incentive for the military at the time of major restructuring of their sources of income. The year of 1998 started a period of almost steady growth of military budget, in comparison with only occasional rapid injections occurring especially after the Gulf War (almost 21 percent in 1992), crisis in the Taiwan Strait (nearly 11 percent in 1996) or later, in response to worsening relations with the United States following an EP-3 plane incident in 2001. General trends in Chinese military financing are presented in the table and chart below. However, the real amount of money spent on the PLA remains a matter of controversy; data estimated by international institutions such as SIPRI are continuously about 1.7–1.8 times China's officially announced military budget,[38] while the US Department of Defense calculates 'China Expenditure Low Estimate' and 'China Expenditure High Estimate' as twice or even three times higher than their official announcements, respectively.[39] US DoD eagerly speculates that most of

---

[36] *Law of the People's Republic of China on Officers in Active Service*, Military Laws and Regulations, http://english.chinamil.com.cn/site2/special-reports/2006-06/19/content_503650.htm (February 2, 2012).

[37] *Decision of the Standing Committee of the National People's Congress on Amending the Regulations of the Chinese People's Liberation Army on the Military Service of Officers in Active Service*, Military Laws and Regulations, http://english.chinamil.com.cn/site2/special-reports/2006-04/19/content_459140.htm (February 2, 2012).

[38] Shaoguang, *The Military Expenditure of China, 1989–98*, in: *SIPRI Yearbook 1999: Armaments, Disarmament and International Security*, Oxford: Oxford University Press, 1999, p. 349.

[39] *Annual Report on Military Power of the People's Republic of China...*, p. 32.

these additional funds have been spent on new armaments which are the key factor of the PLA's modernisation.[40] In general observation, though, a switch to the state-founded military budget has assured a stable income for the PLA, and strengthened the army's loyalty to China as a whole.

Table 1. China's military expenditure 1989–2008 (value in constant 2005 USD millions, change in percent)

Year	Military expenditure	Change year to year
1989	12,276	X
1990	13,147	7.10
1991	13,691	4.14
1992	16,534	20.77
1993	15,331	-7.28
1994	14,607	-4.72
1995	14,987	2.60
1996	16,606	10.80
1997	16,799	1.16
1998	19,263	14.67
1999	21,626	12.27
2000	23,767	9.90
2001	28,515	19.98
2002	33,436	17.26
2003	36,405	8.88
2004	40,631	11.61
2005	44,911	10.53
2006	52,199	16.23
2007	57,861	10.85
2008	63,643	9.99

Source: Calculations based on: *The SIPRI Military Expenditure Database*, The Stockholm International Peace Research Institute, http://milexdata.sipri.org/result.php4 (February 4, 2012).

[40] *Ibid.*, p. 33.

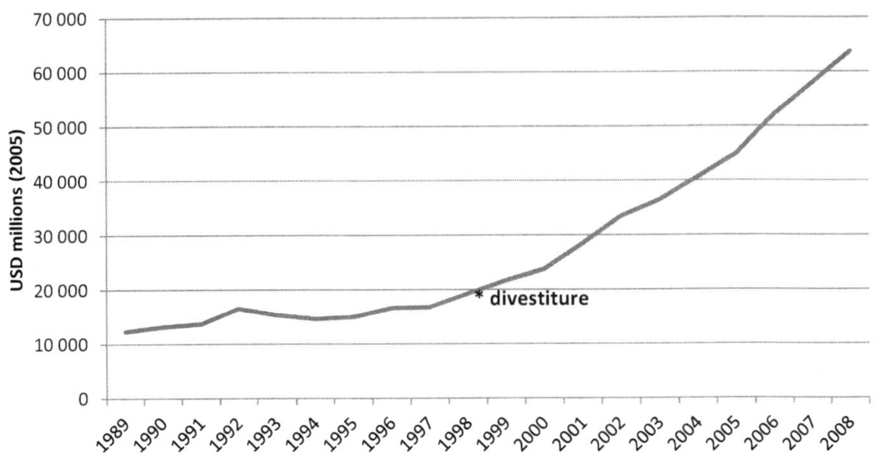

Figure 1. China's military expenditure 1989–2008 (value in constant 2005 USD millions)

Source: Calculations based on: *The SIPRI Military Expenditure Database*, The Stockholm International Peace Research Institute, http://milexdata.sipri.org/result.php4 (February 4, 2012).

A short look on the institutional layer of civil-military relations in China unveils their local characteristics. The Central Military Commission (CMC), which is an organ of the CCP, remains the paramount body governing the army in today's PRC. Even though the Constitution of 1982 introduced the state Central Military Commission, both these military bodies are composed of the same officials and effectively duplicate each other's works; consequently, one can easily acknowledge the existence of both CMC-s, but functioning of only the Party one. This nominal division serves only as a cover for CCP's strict control over the military.[41] CMC works as the core political leadership of the PLA, and coordinates the entire spectrum of national defence policy.[42] CMC is formally led by the General Secretary of the CCP (and concurrently the President of the PRC), but its day-to-day duties are supervised by the powerful and influential Vice-Chairman.[43] In contrast, the actual role of the Ministry of National Defence (MND) in administering the armed forces looks much weaker, especially in comparison with Western, civil-led and publicly controlled national defence bureaucracies. MND is traditionally led by a PLA general who at the same time serves as a member of the CMC. The Ministry's role is limited to organising foreign representation of the military.[44] More powers were given to the State Council (the government

[41] Paltiel, *op. cit.*, p. 786.

[42] Cheung, *op. cit.*, p. 62–63, 68.

[43] Shambaugh, *The Changing of the Guard...*, p. 90–96; Cheung, *op. cit.*, p. 71–73.

[44] Cheung, *op. cit.*, p. 86; Kenneth W. Allen, "*China's Foreign Military Relations with Asia-Pacific,*" *Journal of Contemporary China*, Vol. 10, 2001, p. 653.

of the PRC), including preparation of national defence budget and administration of military resources.[45] To sum up, the Party circles clearly retain the most profound influence on the functioning of the military; state organs as such still seem to be undervalued.

Conclusions

Contemporary relations between the military and the civilian sector in China are at a stage that incomparable to anything before. Some most distinct conclusions are especially worth pointing out. First, even though the PLA does not determine the issues of political succession any longer, the military has retained a considerable power within the country's politics. Despite the fact that the matter of who becomes a paramount leader of the PRC is no longer decided with a crucial approval of the army, it is still not possible to succeed this post completely without the PLA's support.[46] Second, one may not overestimate the range of political change in China; a one-party system must rely on military power, even though the latter is becoming assigned to duties more and more resembling those known on Western grounds. The Party still controls the gun, regardless some occasional ambiguities. The next paramount succession scheduled for 2012 will be a major indicator of the tendency describing the army's involvement in politics. Time will show whether the PLA, with its alleged enormous progress in professionalization, is able to accept a new generation of leaders, again deprived of any significant military credentials. Third, even though any political engagement of the army would interfere with its modernisation trends, the PLA remains a sentinel of CCP's unity and PRC's integrity.[47] A threat to these supreme values can trigger generals' actions in the future; a more capable PLA will likely serve well as a country defender in the time of peril.[48] Will it support the Party in case of any major future internal turmoil, though? This question remains open. Fourth, in terms of the shaping of PRC's foreign and security policy, the military's influence is a function of its capabilities and doctrine. Whenever PLA's actions are entwined with the main objective of China's Grand Strategy: *The Great Renaissance of the Chinese Nation* (*Zhonghua minzu weida fuxing*), the army serves as a tool of national policy. As in the Clausewitzian logic of political ends and adequate means, the military or

[45] Cheung, *op. cit.*, p. 88–89.

[46] Anthony Saich, *Governance and Politics of China*, Houndmills: Palgrave Macmillan, 2004, p. 150.

[47] Joffe, *op. cit.*, p. 20.

[48] *Ibidem*; Anthony Saich, *op. cit.*, p. 151.

gradually assigned to executing orders of the state rather than the Party, and acting in the interest of the former. This delicate issue of allegiance has become a distinct feature of civil-military relations in today's China.

Bibliograhy

Allen Kenneth W., "China's Foreign Military Relations with Asia-Pacific," *Journal of Contemporary China*, Vol. 10, 2001.

Annual Report on Military Power of the People's Republic of China, The US Secretary of Defense, 2008.

Bickford Thomas J., *The People's Liberation Army and Its Changing Economic Roles. Implications for Civil-Military Relations*, in: *Chinese Civil-Military Relations. The Transformation of the People's Liberation Army*, ed. by Li Nan, London: Routledge, 2006.

Blasko Dennis J., *The Chinese Army Today: Tradition and Transformation of the 21st* Century, Abingdon: Routledge, 2006.

Cheung Tai Ming, *The Influence of the Gun: China's CMC and Its Relationship with the Military, Party, and State Decision-Making Systems*, in: David M. Lampton, *The Making of Chinese Foreign and Security Policy in the Era of Reform*, Stanford: Stanford University Press, 2001.

Decision of the Standing Committee of the National People's Congress on Amending the Regulations of the Chinese People's Liberation Army on the Military Service of Officers in Active Service, Military Laws and Regulations, http://english.chinamil.com.cn/site2/special-reports/2006-04/19/content_459140.htm (February 2, 2012).

Dreyer June Teufel, *China's Political System: Modernization and Tradition*, New York: Pearson Education, 2008.

Fewsmith Joseph, *China Since Tiananmen: From Deng Xiaoping to Hu Jintao*, Cambridge: Cambridge University Press, 2008.

Harding Harry, *The Role of the Military in Chinese Politics*, in: *Citizens and Groups in Contemporary China*, ed. Falkenheim Victor C., Ann Arbor: University of Michigan Center for Chinese Studies, 1987.

Joffe Ellis, *The Chinese Army in Domestic Politics. Factors and Phases*, in: *Chinese Civil-Military Relations. The Transformation of the People's Liberation Army*, ed. by Li Nan, London: Routledge, 2006.

Law of the People's Republic of China on Officers in Active Service, Military Laws and Regulations, http://english.chinamil.com.cn/site2/specialreports/200606/19/content_503650.htm (February 2, 2012).

Military Service Law of the People's Republic of China, Military Laws and Regulations, http://english.chinamil.com.cn/site2/special-reports/2006-04/20/content_460092.htm (February 2, 2012).

Mulvenon James C., *Straining Against the Yoke? Civil-Military Relations in China After the Seventeenth Party Congress*, in: *China's Changing Political Land-*

scape: Prospects for Democracy, ed. by Li Cheng, Washington: Brookings Institution Press, 2008.

Paltiel Jeremy T., "PLA Allegiance on Parade: Civil-Military Relations in Transition," *The China Quarterly*, Vol. 143, 1995.

Saich Anthony, *Governance and Politics of China*, Houndmills: Palgrave Macmillan, 2004.

Shambaugh David, "Civil-Military Relations in China: Party-Army or National Military?," *Copenhagen Journal of Asian Studies*, Vol. 16, 2002.

Shambaugh David, *Modernizing China's Military: Progress, Problems and Prospects*, Berkeley: University of California Press, 2002.

Shambaugh David, *The Changing of the Guard: China's New Military Leadership*, in: Chu Yun-han, Lo Chih-cheng and Myers Ramon H., *The New Chinese Leadership: Challenges and Opportunities after the 16th Party Congress*, Cambridge: Cambridge University Press, 2004.

The SIPRI Military Expenditure Database, The Stockholm International Peace Research Institute, http://milexdata.sipri.org/result.php4 (February 4, 2012).

Wang James C.F., *Contemporary Chinese Politics: An Introduction*, New York: Prentice Hall, Upper Saddle River, 2002.

Wang Shaoguang, *The Military Expenditure of China, 1989–98*, in: *SIPRI Yearbook 1999: Armaments, Disarmament and International Security*, Oxford: Oxford University Press, 1999.

You Ji, *Sorting Out the Myths About Political Commissars*, in: *Chinese Civil-Military Relations. The Transformation of the People's Liberation Army*, ed. Li Nan, London: Routledge, 2006.

Chapter Six

Tobiasz Targosz

Chinese Involvement in Southeast Asia on the Example of Myanmar

After the *coup d'etat* in 1988, the military junta, that had seized the power, changed the name of the country from Burma into the historical, Burmese language name Burmese language – the Union of Myanmar. This new name is not acknowledged by most opposition groups, who believe that the regime lacks the legality to engage in any government function, including changing the name of the country. In this article I shall use the old and a new name of this state alternatively.

China's cultural, economical, and political relationships with Southeast Asia have made important pattern of this region. However until the late 19th century, the tributary system dominated Chinese relations with Southeast Asia. In the 20th century, after World War II, when the policy of new postcolonial states was overfilled with the spirit of Bandung Conference , this ancient pattern of mutual relations rapidly changed. In 19th century, after the Second World War, when the policy of new postcolonial states, was overfilled with the spirit of Bandung Conference. Ideas and values like nonalignment, neutrality, mutual respect and equality in political relations made a good background for the developing Chinese relationship with Southeast Asia. Nowadays, this relations is undergoing a significant shift. In the 1990s, China was perceived as a threat to its Southeast Asian neighbors partly due to its conflicting territorial claims over the South China Sea and former support for communist revolts. This perception began to change in the wake of the Asian financial crisis of 1997/1998[1] when China resisted the pressure to devalue its currency, while the currencies of its neighbors were in free fall. In November 2004,

[1] See: Bruce Vaughn, Wayne M. Morrison, *China-Southeast Asia Relations: Trends, Issues, and Implications for the United States*, CRS Report for Congress, April 4, 2006.

China and the Association of Southeast Asian Nations (ASEAN) agreed to gradually remove tariffs and create the world's largest free trade area by 2010.[2] China is also beginning to increase bilateral and multilateral security relationships with Southeast Asian states.

In ancient times the Chinese regarded Myanmar as a 'barbarian' kingdom which wasn't included within the 'civilized' countries that adopted exclusively Chinese culture.[3] After World War II, when the state of Burma gained independence, it attempted to maintain a public stance of neutrality. Especially during the Ne Win's era (began in 1962),[4] this policy of preserving Myanmar's status as a neutral buffer state became a key concept of Myanmar foreign policy. Therefore, when in 1967 the Beijing's embassy in Rangoon began to encourage the local Chinese to participate in the Cultural Revolution, Ne Win's regime prohibited these activities. It soon led to the confrontation with overseas Chinese in Burma and caused a rift in Sino-Burmese relations. Ne Win's skilled personal diplomacy, including a visit to Beijing in 1971,[5] resulted in normalizing the relations between Rangoon and Beijing. Although the Chinese support for the Burma Communistic Party continued to be the main point of Burma's irritation with mutual relations. Until the great Burmese political crisis of 1988, Chinese military's aid for BCP was described as "fraternal party" relations. Since then Beijing cut back on its support for the BCP and began to establish closer relations with, the State Law and Order Restoration Council (SEOK) which seized power in a stage-managed *coup d'etat* on 18th September 1988.[6] The new martial law passed by SEOK opened up the economy to foreign business. The economically weak, politically divided and socially fragmented state of Burma started to search in the world for external sources of economic and military support. Political isolation of the new established military rule in Myanmar, and it's cash-hungry militant government saw China as the main political and economical partner in the region. Even the long-held principles of neutrality and nonalignment in Burmese foreign policy, could not stop this constantly developing process. Furthermore Myanmar soon moved away from a nonalignment policy and has become China's closest ally.

[2] *Agreement on Dispute Settlement Mechanism of the Framework Agreement on Comprehensive Economic Co-Operation Between the Association of Southeast Asian Nations and the People's Republic of China*, http://www.aseansec.org/16635.htm (January 29, 2012).

[3] Donald M. Seekins, "Burma China Relation, Playing with Fire," *Asian Survey*, Vol. 37, No. 6, June 1997.

[4] Michael W. Charney, *A History of Modern Burma*, Cambridge: Cambridge University Press, 2009, p. 107.

[5] Ting Maung Maung, "Myanmar and China. A Special Relationships?," *Southeast Asian Affairs*, 2003, p. 189–210.

[6] *Ibid.*

According to Donald M. Seekins "by the mid-1990s until now, Myanmar seemed to be drawn increasingly into a Chinese sphere of influence."[7]

Myanmar calls China the "Paukhpaw," a term that means 'sibling' or 'intimate' in Burmese.[8] Moreover, this word has never been used for any other foreign country. It is a proof of a strong historical and political connection between those two nations. Although, most important thing is that this perception of its neighbor in past, same as in the present, has undergone a series of ups and downs. In the past such events like the invasion of Mongols army in the 13th century, which destroyed the first unified Burmese kingdom, and the invasion of Qing's army in the 18th century evoked a strong distrust and resentment in the minds of the designers of Myanmar's foreign policy.[9] However after the *coup d'etat* when the military junta made a transition from socialistic economy in the era of Ne Win into free market system, historical resentment has become less important than economical interests which is beneficial for the military junta. The State Law and Order Restoration Council used foreign business to consolidate military rule, but not to: "promote economic growth or industrialization"[10] in the state. This attitude in economy has a long historical tradition, according to Robert Taylor: "the experience of the monarchical system in Burma was such as to convince kings that they would be unable to control the private power which would probably have resulted from economic expansion and rationalization, even if this would have increased the overall resource base of society and ultimately the state."[11] According to this pre-colonial pattern which exists in the present, economic, military and political relations with China soon became the main source of support and legitimacy of the Myanmar junta.

In economical relations the Chinese position can be seen as a dominant. According to Thai source from 1995, Sino-Burmese two-way trade in 1994–1995 amounted to 1.2 billion USD, or 60 percent of Burma's total trade.[12] It made China the major trade partner for the Union of Myanmar. This growing development of bilateral trade relations shows a growing asymmetry since 1988. It is evident that Myanmar's import from China grew more rapidly than its export to China throughout the 1990s and up to 2005. Myanmar's exports to China increased 1.3 times, from 133.7 million USD in 1988 to 169.4 million USD in 2003 its import from China

[7] Seekins, *op. cit.*

[8] Toshiro Kudo, *Myanmar Economic Relations with China: Can China Support the Myanmar Economy?*, Institute of Developing Countries, Discussion Paper No. 66, July 2006.

[9] *China's Myanmar Dilemma*, International Crisis Group, Asia Report No. 177, September 14, 2009.

[10] Seekins, *op. cit.*

[11] Robert H. Taylor, *The State in Burma*, Honolulu: University of Hawaii Press, 1987, p. 38.

[12] Seekins, *op. cit.*

increased 7.1 times, from 136.2 million USD in 1988 to 967.2 million USD in 2003, resulting in a huge trade deficit of 797.7 million USD in 2003.[13] Also the Chinese economic presence, which is most visible in the central and northern part of the country – the Upper Burma – and in the frontier region along the Burma-China border adjacent to Yunnan Province, becomes more and more unbalanced year by year. Mandalay, Burma's second largest city, could be a good example of this regularity. The city enjoyed a great development due to the Chinese activity in land purchase. But soon it became obvious to the local Burmese that commercial center of this old royal city became the so-called 'Chinatown,' where prices of property had become too high for the Burmese to afford. It forced the Burmese citizens to move to the city's outskirts.

On the Chinese side of the border, districts like Yingjiang, and Lungchuang, Tengchung in Yunnan Province gain profits form bilateral trade. To support this trade Beijing has given the towns of Wanding and Ruili on the Burma-China border a special open city status. The area neighboring on Ruili has been designated as a 'special economic development zone.' In the shadow of this progress stands an enormous growth of border drug trade which throughout Yunann, has been affecting the whole China since the 80s. Burma serves as a passageway for opium and heroin, and most recently also for amphetamine type stimulant, from the 'Gold Triangle.' The center of opium and heroin production is located in the Kokang region in the northeast of Burma. According to David Arnott: "most of the drug warlords in Burma were either born in China, are ethnic Chinese, or of Chinese/Burmese parentage."[14] One of them was Ma Siling who was arrested after a secret operation of the Chinese police in his fortified villa in Pingyuan. He kept 981 kilograms of drugs there, along with a huge number of various weapons and his private army of 854 people.[15] Nowadays drug trade form Myanmar to the People's Republic of China causes a huge number of social problems for the Chinese government, especially in border provinces like Yunnan. The most significant is the growing number of drug users in this province which increased from 1.7 percent in 2004 to 11.1 percent in 2007 also during this time the age of narcotics users dropped rapidly.[16] Since in Myanmar: "narcotics have be-

---

[13] Kudo, *op. cit.*

[14] See: David Arnott, *China – Burma Relations*, in: *Challenges to Democratization in Burma: Perspectives on multilateral and bilateral responses*, International Institute for Democracy and Electoral Assistance (International IDEA) 2001, p. 69–86, http://www.idea.int/asia_pacific/burma/upload/challenges_to_democratization_in_burma.pdf (June 28, 2012).

[15] Bertil Linter, *Drugs and Economic Growth. Ethnicity and Exports*, in: *Burma: Prospects for Democratic Future*, ed. Robert I. Rotberg, Washington D.C.: Brookings Institution Press, 1998, p. 173.

[16] *China's Myanmar Dilemma...*

come the country's single most important export"[17] there are no prospects for a change. Especially that many corrupted Chinese officials have been involved in this drug business.

The other stage of economic relations between China and Myanmar is the Chinese cooperation in mining, oil, gas, hydropower and infrastructure. According to the research made by nongovernmental EarthRights International (ERI) in Myanmar there are at least 69 Chinese multinational corporations involved in at least 90 hydropower, oil and natural gas, and mining projects in Burma.[18] Chinese corporations have been involved in 63 hydropower projects including the largest 7,100 megawatt Tasang Dam on the Salween River,[19] is going to be integrated into the Asian Development Bank's Greater Mekong Sub-region Power Grid in the future. What is interesting in this project is that most of the electricity is destined for export to the neighboring Thailand.[20] In the Kachin State, several Chinese MNCs are involved in the construction of seven large dams along the N'Mai Hka, Mali Hka, and Irrawaddy River, according to the agreement signed in 2007 between China Power Investment Co. and Myanmar authorities.[21] China is also involved in mining industries and gas and oil companies. Mining is often located in areas where access is restricted, so our knowledge about this type of Chinese projects is very poor. According to foreign researchers the most important sphere of the Chinese influence in Burma is the Chinese activity in exploitations of oil, natural gas and also construction of pipelines. The longest pipeline, which is now being constructed, will lead from Kyaukphyu to Kunming or Chongqing. In the future this and other pipelines would help China facilitate import of oil and natural gas from the Middle East, South America and Africa. It has a strategic meaning for China resource safety during the time when transport through Malacca Straits is dangerous because of piracy.

Chinese military assistance in Burma has begun since the visit of Generals Khin Nyunt and Than Shwe to Beijing in October 1989.[22] After this visit SLORC purchased as much as 1 billion USD worth of weapons from China, which is the largest arms deal in Burma's history. These weapons included fighter aircrafts, patrol boats, tanks, armored personnel carriers, missiles, anti-aircraft guns, and trucks. China soon became the larg-

[17] Linter, *op. cit.*, p. 178.

[18] *China in Burma: The Increasing Investment of Chinese Multinational Corporations in Burma's Hydropower, Oil and Natural Gas, and Mining Sectors*, Earth Right Organization, September 2008, http://www.burmalibrary.org/docs5/China_in_Burma-ERI.pdf (June 28, 2012).

[19] *Ibid.*

[20] *Ibid.*

[21] *China in Burma..., op. cit.*

[22] Marvin C. Ott, *From Isolation to Relevance. Policy Considerations*, in: *Burma: Prospects for Democratic Future...*, p. 72.

est supplier of arms to Burma. However, in the mid 1990s, the generals diversified their weapons suppliers, which was a response to dissatisfaction with the quality of Chinese military weaponry.[23] Myanmar authorities also believe that it would be better to rely on various sources if the main supplier cut them off. Chinese assistance in the construction of military facilities that could pave the way for a significant Chinese presence in the Indian Ocean according to Andrew Selth flourish in: "a steady stream of newspaper stories, scholarly monographs and books that have referred inter alia to the existence of Chinese military bases in Burma" which only a few: "drew on hard evidence or gave verifiable sources to support their claims."[24] When in 2005, the Chairman of the Indian Defence Force's Chiefs of Staff Committee announced that reports of a Chinese intelligence facility on one of Burma's offshore islands were incorrect and that there were no Chinese naval bases in Burma, scholars became more skeptical about the Chinese military presence in Myanmar.[25] Now it is certain that claims about China's influence in Burma over the past 15 years have been greatly exaggerated.

Because of the 'Malacca Dilemma' China has developed port facilities in the cities stretching from the South China Sea through the Straits of Malacca, across the Indian Ocean, and towards the Persian Gulf. Ports in Hainggyi, Coco, Sittwe, Zadetkyi Kyun, Myeik and Kyaukphyu became a part of the Chinese 'string of pearls' system.[26] Their main aim is to protect Chinese oil shipments. In these ports China provided assistance in the construction of radar, communications upgrade, and refueling facilities.

Another important factor in bilateral relations is the Chinese pressure on Burmese ethnic minority. China is trying to prevent Myanmar's ethnic groups from gaining full autonomy. China fears that such precedent could rouse nationalist views among the groups on its side of the boundary. Especially that most of this groups along the border areas of China and Myanmar are related, such as the Shan and Yunnan's Dai people, the Kachin and Yunnan's Jinpo people, and the Wa on both sides of the border.[27] Chinese authorities have also been active in assisting SLORC to make ceasefire agreements with border insurgents, especially the Kachin Independence Organization, which are one of the best-organized, best equipped and most motivated ethnic rebel group.[28] However, a ceasefire

[23] *China's Myanmar Dilemma...*

[24] Andrew Selth, *Chinese Military Bases in Burma: The Explosion of a Myth*, The Griffith Asia Institute, Regional Outlook Paper No. 10, 2007.

[25] *China's Myanmar Dilemma...*

[26] *Ibid.*

[27] *Ibid.*

[28] Ardeth Maung Thawnghmung, *The Karen Revolution in Burma: Diverse Voices, Uncertain Ends*, Singapore: East West Center, 2008, p. IX.

agreement is not the final solution to Burma's current rising political problem connected with minorities insurgencies. It also cannot stabilize the situation on the Chin-Burma border side which is greatly desired by China. China is trying to use its relationships with ethnic groups as a buffer and leverage in managing its relationship with the government. For example China's closest relationship is with the Wa, who has the largest army. It caused a discontent of the Myanmar militant regime.[29] Although this pattern in bilateral, China-Myanmar relationships will not change in the near future or they even will not change at all. The Chinese aims are first of all pragmatic. Good relations with both the junta's government and various insurgent movements can easily enable China's access into strategic sources placed in the areas occupied by the government and ethnic minorities armies.

Nowadays, Myanmar-China relation becomes the main cause of frustration and dissatisfaction for Beijing. China reaction to the Saffron Revolution in 2007 and then a year later in May, when the military junta denied the access for national aid agencies and aid workers to the victims of the Cyclone Nargis, shows Beijing's great discontent. From Beijing's point of view, especially in 2008, the timing could not have been worse, just three months before the Olympics. Furthermore this crisis did not change anything in the attitude of the junta's generals. The government in Naypyidaw is intensely nationalistic and resistant to foreign interference. It does not have a rational perception of foreigners and international relations. General Than Shwe, who played the main role in policy making, is considered to be particularly unpredictable and superstitious, similar to one of his great predecessors Gen. Ne Win[30]. The military regime is capricious, unreliable and suffers from the lack of transparency. Its decision to relocate the capital to Naypyidaw in November 2005 caused consternation and anger in Beijing.[31] A similar situation took place when Gen. Khin Nyunt's proChina policy led to doubts about his loyalty and ended in his elimination. Until that, the Chinese leaders believed that Khin Nyunt could have become a statesman and they called him 'Deng Xiaoping of Burma.'[32] Burma's geostrategic position makes this country the most important part of the Chinese strategy directed to Southeast Asia. Myanmar is also important in the context of being for China the a key to revive its 'southwest silk road', which origi-

[29] *China's Myanmar Dilemma...*

[30] See: David Martin Jones, *The Southeast Asia Development Model. Non-Liberal Democracy with Market Accountability*, Southeast Asian Affairs, 2007; Diane Mahler, *Than Shwe's Burma*, Minneapolis: Twenty First Century Books, 2010, p. 73.

[31] *China's Myanmar Dilemma...*

[32] *Ibid...*

nally led from the Yunnan Province to Myanmar and westward to Bangladesh, India and the West. However Myanmar has posed an increasing challenge to China's global diplomacy and international image with its irresponsible political behavior. In my opinion, Myanmar's strong sense of nationalism and its determination to preserve its independence and cultural identity, guarantee that it will not become a 'Chinese puppet' like some scholars would like to see it. But without Chinese political and economical help, especially long-term loans with low interest rates the Myanmar government could not resist an internal political crisis. Strengthened economic ties with China are for the regime a chance to survive economic sanctions of Western nations. China's policy towards Myanmar is based on the principles established at the Bandung Conference. The principles are: mutual respect for sovereignty and territorial integrity, mutual non-aggression, non-interference in each other's internal affairs, equality and mutual benefit, and peaceful coexistence.[33] From China's point of view, which is based on its past experience, sanctions punish people more than governments. Rejecting tactics of isolation and sanctions in case of Myanmar is connected with Beijing's belief that political change must be gradual and is best promoted by engagement and encouraging economic development. However, Chinese assistance will not be a powerful force promoting the process of broad-based economic development in Myanmar. Burma's relationship with China preserves an incompetent and repressive order, and puts the country in economic and political stagnation. On the other side of the border, Burma stands in the Chinese perspective, in the way of regional development and is the main 'exporter' of HIV/AIDS and drugs to China.[34]

China's support for the military regime in Burma has had negative consequences for both countries. However, geostrategic interests of the both countries are currently stronger than disadvantages of these relationships. Due to the different scenarios the situation in Burma can develop in various ways. According to the most pessimistic, Myanmar is playing with fire, seeking closer military, strategic and economic ties with China. It can lead the state into a quasi colonial dependence on China and Rangoon will become a strategic satellite base for China, like it was for the British Empire 150 years ago. However according to Poon

[33] See: See Seng Tan, Amitav Acharya, *Bandung Revisited Offers a Critical Reassessment of the Intellectual, Social, and Political Legacies of the 1955 Asian-African Conference by Drawing on Research in Area Studies, Diplomatic History, and International Relations*, Singapore: National University of Singapore, 2008, p. 13, 135; Pobzeb Vang, *Five Principles of Chinese Foreign Policies*, Bloomington: AuthorHouse, 2008, p. 32.

[34] Poon Kim Shee, "The Political Economy of China-Myanmar Relations: Strategic and Economic Dimensions," *Ritsumeikan Annual Review of International Studies*, The International Studies Association of Ritsumeikan University, Vol. 1, 2002, p. 33–53.

Kim Shee: "Sino-Myanmar ties are uneven, asymmetrical but nevertheless reciprocal and mutually beneficial" and the entente is not a tributary relationship but rather "a marriage of convenience."[35]

Bibliography

Agreement on Dispute Settlement Mechanism of the Framework Agreement on Comprehensive Economic Co-Operation Between the Association of Southeast Asian Nations and the People's Republic of China, http://www.aseansec.org/16635.htmm (January 29, 2012).

Arnott David, *China-Burma Relations*, in: *Challenges to Democratization in Burma: Perspectives on multilateral and bilateral responses*, International Institute for Democracy and Electoral Assistance (International IDEA) 2001, http://www.idea.int/asia_pacific/burma/upload/challenges_to_democratization_in_burma.pdf (June 28, 2012).

Charney Michael W., *A History of Modern Burma*, Cambridge: Cambridge University Press, 2009.

China in Burma: The increasing investment of Chinese Multinational corporations in Burma's hydropower, oil and natural gas, and mining sectors, Earth Right Organization, September 2008, http://www.burmalibrary.org/docs5/China_in_Burma-ERI.pdf (June 28, 2012).

China's Myanmar Dilemma, International Crisis Group, Asia Report No. 177, September 14, 2009.

Jones David Martin, *The Southeast Asia Development Model. Non-Liberal Democracy with Market Accountability*, Southeast Asian Affairs, 2007.

Kim Shee Poon, "The Political Economy of China-Myanmar Relations: Strategic and Economic Dimensions," *Ritsumeikan Annual Review of International Studies*, The International Studies Association of Ritsumeikan University, Vol. 1, 2002.

Kudo Toshiro, *Myanmar Economic Relations with China: Can China Support the Myanmar Economy?*, Institute of Developing Countries, Discussion Paper No. 66, July 2006.

Linter Bertil, *Drugs and Economic Growth. Ethnicity and Exports*, in: *Burma: Prospects for Democratic Future*, ed. by Robert I. Rotberg, Washington D.C.: Brookings Institution Press, 1998.

Mahler Diane, *Than Shwe's Burma*, Minneapolis: Twenty First Century Books, 2010.

Maung Maung Ting, "Myanmar and China. A Special Relationships?," *Southeast Asian Affairs*, 2003.

Maung Thawnghmung Ardeth, *The Karen Revolution in Burma: Diverse Voices, Uncertain Ends*, Singapore: East West Center, 2008.

[35] *Ibid.*

Ott Marvin C., *From Isolation to Relevance. Policy Considerations*, in: *Burma: Prospects for Democratic Future*, ed. by Robert I. Rotberg, Washington D.C.: Brookings Institution Press, 1998.

Seng Tan See, Amitav Acharya, *Bandung Revisited Offers a Critical Reassessment of the Intellectual, Social, and Political Legacies of the 1955 Asian-African Conference by Drawing on Research in Area Studies, Diplomatic History, and International Relations*, Singapore: National University of Singapore, 2008.

Seekins Donald M., "Burma China Relation, Playing with Fire," *Asian Survey*, Vol. 37, No. 6, June 1997.

Selth Andrew, *Chinese Military Bases in Burma: The Explosion of a Myth*, The Griffith Asia Institute, Regional Outlook Paper No. 10, 2007.

Taylor Robert H., *The State in Burma*, Honolulu: University of Hawaii Press, 1987.

Vang Pobzeb, *Five Principles of Chinese Foreign Policies*, Bloomington: AuthorHouse, 2008.

Vaughn Bruce, Morrison Wayne M., *China-Southeast Asia Relations: Trends, Issues, and Implications for the United States*, CRS Report for Congress, April 4, 2006.

Chapter Seven

Anna Kotfis

China's Energy Policy towards Central Asia and Russia

China's thirty-year economic development caused a huge hunger for energy. During this period, began by Deng Xiaoping's Four Modernizations, the People's Republic of China became the second largest energy consumer after the United States. The country's energy security is the most important dimension of Chinese national security. Despite the economic slowdown in exports and domestic demand in 2009, China's demand for energy remains high.[1] According to long-term prognosis, there will be a systematic increase of crude oil and natural gas in China's energy balance. But due to its limited natural resources, Beijing is forced to seek them abroad.[2] Unprecedented demand for imported resources is currently a major factor that is shaping the Chinese foreign policy.[3]

Table 1. Projected energy demand in China

Year	2010	2015	2020
Total (billion tons of coal equivalent)	1.70	1.88	2.01
Oil (percent)	27.5	28.9	31.30
Gas (percent)	7.4	9.4	12.00

Source: Łukasz Gacek, "Oil In Chinese Foreign Policy," in: *Acta Asiatica Varsoviensia*, ed. by Roman M. Sławiński, No. 22, Polish Academy of Science, Centre for Studies on Non-European Countries, 2009.

[1] Edward Haliżak, *Polityka i strategia Chin w kształtowaniu międzynarodowego bezpieczeństwa*, Żurawia Papers, Issue 10, Warszawa: Wydawnictwo Naukowe Scholar, 2007, p. 124–125; U.S. Energy Information Administration, http://www.eia.gov/countries/cab.cfm?fips=CH (March 19, 2012).

[2] See: Łukasz Gacek, "Oil In Chinese Foreign Policy," in: *Acta Asiatica Varsoviensia*, ed. Roman M. Sławiński, No. 22, Polish Academy of Science, Centre for Studies on Non-European Countries, 2009.

[3] Haliżak, *op. cit.*, p. 124.

Cooperation with Central Asia

Central Asia is one of the regions where China seeks natural resources. But two decades ago, when new independent countries were established, after Soviet Union's collapse, it was not as obvious as it is now. The emergence of new states, Kazakhstan, Kyrgyzstan, Tajikistan, Turkmenistan and Uzbekistan, led to fundamental changes in the geopolitical landscape of Eurasia. In the 19th century, Central Asia was the arena of the 'Great Game' in which the Tsarist Russia and the British Empire struggled for strategic primacy. Today, the US, Russia, and China are competing for similar supremacy in the region.[4] To describe this situation, journalists and analysts specializing in Central Asia revisited the term. The present competition in the region is also often referred to as the 'New Great Game.'[5] In the early 1990s maintaining stability in Xinjiang and resolving the border dispute with Russia and Central Asian countries was at the top of the Chinese agenda. Subsequently another issues, like energy cooperation, became important factors in China's strategic calculus.[6] Thanks to growing engagement since the start of the 2000s, the People's Republic of China has become an increasingly important player on the Central Asian scene, which until then, was essentially divided between Russia and the US.[7]

Central Asia, due to its location between Russia, China, the Indian subcontinent and Middle East, is a region of a strategic importance. The main reason that the region is so attractive to great powers is the abundance of resources, especially natural gas and oil. Kazakhstan's proven oil reserves are the ninth largest in the world, and in terms of gas reserves, Turkmenistan with over 4 percent of the world's proven reserves, is the leader in the region. While the reserves of oil and gas in the Central Asia region are difficult to access given their landlocked nature, the tightness of oil global markets has nevertheless boosted their value.[8] Given this facts, the current China's Central Asia strategy is determined by the issue of energy.

[4] Ramakant Dwivedi, "China's Central Asia Policy In Recent Times," *The China and Eurasia Forum Quarterly*, Central Asia-Caucasus Institute, Silk Road Studies Program, Vol. 4, No. 4, 2006, p. 140.

[5] Aleksandra Jaroszewicz, Maciej Falkowski, *The Great Game around Turkmenistan*, Warsaw: Publisher Centre for Eastern Studies, August 2008, p. 7, http://www.osw.waw.pl/sites/default/files/punkt_widzenia_17.pdf (February 2, 2012).

[6] Dwivedi, *op. cit.*, p. 140.

[7] See: Sébastien Peyrouse, "Central Asia's growing partnership with China," *EUCAM Working Paper*, EUCAM EU-Central Asia Monitoring, No. 4, October 2009.

[8] John Seaman, *Energy Security, Transnational Pipelines and China's Role in Asia*, IFRI Centre Asie, April 2010, p. 23.

Table 2. Oil and gas proved reserves in Cetral Asian key countries

Country	Gas (trillion cubic metres)	Oil (million barrels)
Turkmenistan	8.10	0.6
Kazakhstan	1.82	39.8
Uzbekistan	1.68	0.6

Source: *BP Statistical Review of World Energy 2010.*

Beijing looks to Central Asia to reduce its energy deficit, diversify its energy imports and transit routes, and increase its energy security. From the Beijing's perspective active policy towards Central Asian states has two main advantages. First, China tries to deal with the problem called "Malacca Strait's Dilemma". Eighty percent of imported oil goes to China through this narrow stretch of water[9] separating peninsular Malaysia from the Indonesian island of Sumatra. This is an extremely vulnerable transit route for China, for if it was cut off, much of the country's oil supplies could be blocked. In the event of conflict, it would be easy for the United States or even India to disrupt China's energy supplies by imposing a naval blockade of this strait. One of the solutions for Bejing, apart from developing sea power, is to diversify its network of transit routes, also via Central Asia. Secondly, reliance on a few energy exporters in the Middle East makes the People's Republic of China vulnerable to political disputes in this volatile region. For the above reason, China is seeking to diversify its energy imports, also by cooperation with Central Asia.[10]

China and Turkmenistan

Turkmenistan, thanks to its abundant gas resources is often called the country of natural gas.[11] Indeed, proved reserves of this raw material are the biggest in Central Asia, causing a struggle for access to them. Chinese policy towards Ashhabad is largely determined by energy interests, what is expressed especially in Turkmenistan-China gas pipeline project. According to the plan, it was launched in December 2009 during the president Hu Jintao's visit in Turkmenistan. The new, 4350-mile long pipeline, which was built very quickly, will eventually import up to

[9] Hongyi Lai, "China Builds Bridges to Fuel Its Engine Room," *Financial Times*, July 4, 2010.

[10] Niklas Swanström, "China's Role In Central Asia: Soft and Hard Power," *Global Dialogue*, Vol. 9, No. 1–2, Winter–Spring 2007.

[11] See: Giampaolo R. Capisani, *Nowe państwa Azji Środkowej*, Warszawa: Wydawnictwo Akademickie Dialog, 2004.

40 billion cubic meters when it reaches its full capacity in 2012.[12] Traveling from Turkmen Bagtiyarlik gas fields through Uzbekistan and Kazakhstan and across the People's Republic of China to east and southeast, it is the longest pipeline in the world. The original framework agreement to deliver Turkmen gas via a pipeline was drawn up in 2006, and contracts were signed to supply up to 30 bcm of gas per year from Turkmenistan within a 30 year period. In June 2009, an additional agreement was reached to add 10 bcm more of Turkmen gas per year as a part of China's involvement in the South Yolotan development project. The Turkmenistan-China gas pipeline is part of China's strategy to expand its influence by developing economic cooperation with Central Asia, and building energy infrastructures in the region. Its opening has changed the geopolitical situation in Central Asia almost irreversibly. It has established China as the main player next to Russia, with a stronger position than the European Union. Completion of gas pipeline means that Central Asia became more important for Beijing, which has now strategically important economic interests in the region, so China will be more determined to defend its interests in the region. For Russia, new eastward pipeline marks the failure of its policy to monopolize gas export routes from Central Asia and keep the countries of the region politically dependent on Moscow.[13]

Sino-Kazakh cooperation

Among all Central Asian states Kazakhstan enjoys a unique status. Since 2005 Sino-Kazakh relations have been termed 'strategic,' what means the highest diplomatic status. Beijing perceives Astana as a major partner in the region, and energy stakes make up a key element of their cooooperation. The most important example of energy cooperation between Beijing and Astana is the oil pipeline, running from Atyrau on the Caspian Sea to Chinese Xinjiang. The first agreement was signed in 1997, and at that time it was quite a big surprise, given that Chinese oil investment abroad was at a nascent stage at that time.[14] But after reaching the settlement,

[12] Kevin Rosner, "China Scores Again in Energy: Russia & Central Asia," *Journal of Energy Security*, January 12, 2010, http://www.ensec.org/index.php?option=com_content&view=article&id=230:china-scores-again-in-energy-russia-aamp-central-asia&catid=102:issuecontent&Itemid=355 (February 2, 2012).

[13] Aleksandra Jarosiewicz, *The Turkmenistan-China Gas Pipeline Considerably Strengthens China's Position in Central Asia*, December 16, 2009, Centre for Eastern Studies, http://www.osw.waw.pl/en/publikacje/eastweek/2009-12-16/turkmenistan-china-gas-pipeline-considerably-strengthens-chinas-posit (February 2, 2012); Seaman, *op. cit.*, p. 25–26.

[14] Stanisław Zapaśnik, *Stosunki Chin z republikami Azji Centralnej*, in: *Azja Wschodnia na przełomie XX i XXI w.*, Vol. 2, *Stosunki międzynarodowe i gospodarcze*, ed. by Krzysztof Gawlikowski, Małgorzata Ławacz, ISP PAN, Warszawa: Wydawnictwo TRIO, 2004, p. 60.

hesitations have occured, linked to the long term implications of the project, and the conviction that there may simply not be enough oil to fill it emerged. The situation changed in 2003, when the pipeline plan was reintroduced thanks to a number of factors. The first was the discovery of substantial new oil reserves in Kazakhstan, notably in offshore Kashagan field, and a boost in overall Kazakh oil production (from 536,000 barrels per day in 1997 to 1.3 million in 2004). Moreover, rise in the price of oil on the international market, growing domestic supply shortages, and concerns for the viability of the ESPO pipeline in Russia, induced the People's Republic of China to push the completion of a join Sino-Kazakh project forward. However it was divided into three stages, east middle and west (see table below). The east stage, from Atasu to Alashankou, was launched in 2006 and began to carry 40,000 barrels of oil per day to China.[15] In 2009 the last, middle part of the pipeline, was finished, which gave China the access to Caspian Sea oil fields, where the biggest reserves of Kazakh oil are located, and enable Beijing to increase oil import from Kazakhstan. It will also help the People's Republic of China to more fully implement its plans to diversify oil markets and transport routes. Finally, the completion of the pipeline is also a sign of China's expansion in Central Asia.[16] The People's Republic of China is also interested in Kazakh's oil fields. The general strategy of Beijing is to connect all the acquired fields along the Sino-Kazakh pipeline. In 2006, China was managing approximately 24 percent of Kazakh oil production.[17]

Table 3. Stages of Kazakh-China oil pipeline

	Localization	Year of finishing
East stage	Atasu–Alashankou	2006
Middle stage	Kenkiyak–Atasu	2009
West stage	Atyrau–Kenkiyak	2003

Source: http://www.eia.doe.gov/cabs/Kazakhstan/Oil.html (February 2, 2012).

Recent economic crisis showed that China is the most reliable partner for Kazakhstan. In April 2009, during the visit of Nursultan Nazarbayev

[15] Seaman, *op. cit.*, p. 23–25.

[16] *Kazakhstan Completes Oil Pipeline to China*, July 14, 2009, Centre for Eastern Studies, http://www.osw.waw.pl/en/publikacje/eastweek/2009-07-15/kazakhstan-completes-oil-pipeline-china (February 2, 2012).

[17] Peyrouse, "Sino-Kazakh Relations: A Nascent Strategic Partnership," *China Brief*, The Jamestown Foundation, Vol. 8, Issue 21, November 4, 2008, http://www.jamestown.org/single/?no_cache=1&tx_ttnews[tt_news]=34142 (February 2, 2012); U.S. Energy Information Administration, http://www.eia.gov/emeu/cabs/Kazakhstan/pdf.pdf (March 19, 2012).

in Beijing, both countries signed a few important agreements. Under the terms of contracts, Kazachstan will recive 10 billion USD in total for its energy projects. Half of this amount was lent by China's Export and Import Bank to Development Bank of Kazachstan, and the second half was provided by CNPC to its Kazakh counterpart – KazMunaiGas. The loan from CNPC gave the Chinese oil firms a 50 percent stake (plus two share) in the joint purchase of MangistauMunaiGaz, Kazakhstan's biggest private oil and gas company. The reached settlement is profitable to both countries. As for Kazachstan, Chinese money helped to deal with bad consequences of economic decline, whereas China was assured that the energy projects of strategic importance will be implemented.[18]

China also looks to Kazakh gas market. Not only is Kazakhstan a transit country for Turkmenistan-China gas pipeline, but it also plans to deliver its own natural gas to China. In June 2010, during Hu Jintao's visit to Astana, both countries signed a deal to build and finance a natural gas pipeline. According to CNPC statement, feasibility studies will also be undertaken, looking at increasing gas exports to China from the Caspian Sea area and other Central Asian countries through the pipeline.

In June 2010 China also signed a deal with Uzbekistan to buy 10 billion cubic meters of natural gas per year from the country. Both countries also signed a memorandum of understanding to expand their cooperation on gas.[19]

Cooperation with Russia

Russia possesses has the world's largest proven natural gas reserves and the second largest oil reserves outside of the Middle East. As in the case of Central Asia, joint projects of landing pipelines are the solution for the abovementioned 'Malacca Dilemma' for China. Moreover, transnational pipelines bring the bonus of longer-term economic opportunity to China's flagging northeastern oil producing regions, giving a gradual decline of the Daqing oil field. Whereas Russia is looking to diversify its oil and gas export markets, reducing dependence on European direction.

---

[18] Wenran Jiang, "China makes Strides in Energy «Go-out» Strategy," *China Brief*, The Jamestown Foundation, Vol. 9, Issue 15, July 23, 2009, http://www.jamestown.org/programs/chinabrief/single/?tx_ttnews[tt_news]=35309&tx_ttnews[backPid]=25&cHash=1828d2cfe2 (February 2, 2012); *China is Kazakhstan's Strategic Partner in Times of Crisis*, April 22, 2009, Centre for Eastern Studies, http://www.osw.waw.pl/en/publikacje/eastweek/2009-04-22/china-kazakhstans-strategic-partner-times-crisis (February 2, 2012).

[19] Wan Zhihong, "China, Kazakhstan Sign New Gas Pipeline Deal," *China Daily*, June 14, 2010.

Russia's largest and most underdeveloped oil and gas fields are located in Eastern Siberia, making East Asia, including China, the ideal market for Russian export. As Western Siberia's natural resources continue to decline, new financing from Asian partners for developing fields in the east has become crucial to meeting the country's long-term production targets.[20] Despite these circumstances, energy cooperation between two regional powers was hampered by several factors through the years.

A significant breakthrough in Sino-Russian energy relations occurred already, when the Chinese Prime Minister Wen Jiabao signed in Moscow a settlement in October 2008 which stipulates the construction of a branch of the East Siberia/Pacific Ocean (ESPO) oil pipeline running to Daqing in China, which Beijing had been trying to achieve for several years. In exchange Russian oil firms Rosneft and Transneft reached a 25 billion USD loan agreement with China Development Bank in February 2010. Under their provisions, Russian companies must use Chinese loans for projects related to oil supplies that are going to China, but Rosneft is also permitted to use a part of the loan to repay its debts to other non-Chinese financial institutions. Another two settlements were signed between CNPC and Russian companies, providing oil supplies to 300 mln tons over 20 years, and giving a possibility that ESPO oil pipeline can be materialized in near future.[21] Indeed, in December 2009, the Russian Prime Minister Vladimir Putin opened a new oil export terminal at Kozmino, which will serve as a key gateway for Russian energy exports to Asian markets. Pacific port city of Kozmino is the destination for the EPSO oil pipeline. The history of this energy project begins in 1994, when the Russian side for the first time proposed building a pipeline from Eastern Siberia. It took five years for details to emerge, and in July 2001 a basic agreement was reached. Two years later CNPC and private Russian company Yukos signed an agreement to jointly construct an oil pipeline from Angarsk to Daqing, at that time to China exclusively, not towards the Pacific Ocean. But after a political battle between the Russian President Vladimir Putin and Yukos's head Mikhail Khodorkovsky, which ended in Khodorkovsky's imprisonment and the state's seizure of Yukos, the deal from 2001 was thrown out. Soon, it turned out that the second option of oil's rout came into prominence.[22]

In 2004, the Russian government took a decision to build a pipeline from Taishet in eastern Siberia via Skovorodino near the border with China to the port city of Kozmino on the Pacific, only additionally with

[20] Seaman, *op. cit.*, p. 17.

[21] Jiang, *op. cit.*

[22] Seaman, *op. cit.*, p. 17–20.

a branch to Chinese Daqing.[23] It was a sign that Moscow intended to export oil not only to China, but also to Japan and South Korea or even North America. Nevertheless, the construction of the Daqing's branch was delayed, because the Russian party claimed the lack of previously pledged financing from Beijing.[24] Under these circumstances, recent Moscow's consent to build Daqing's pipeline, without any political concessions from China, marks a new stage of bilateral relations. This stage is becoming dominated by economic items, which are of the greatest importance to Beijing, and Russian side is going to be relatively weaker in bilateral relations.[25]

Conclusions

Due to the constantly growing China's hunger for energy, Russia and Central Asia are becoming more important to Beijing's policy. Energy cooperation with both of them allows China to reduce its energy deficit, diversify its energy imports and transit routes, and increase its energy security. It is worth underlining that both regions, having land border with China, help Beijing cope with a problem called the 'Malacca Dilemma', which means over-reliance on sea transit routes of energy resources.

Bibliography

Capisani Giampaolo R., *Nowe państwa Azji Środkowej*, Warszawa: Wydawnictwo Akademickie Dialog, 2004.

China is Kazakhstan's Strategic Partner in Times of Crisis, April 22, 2009, Centre for Eastern Studies, http://www.osw.waw.pl/en/publikacje/eastweek/2009-04-22/china-kazakhstans-strategic-partner-times-crisis (February 2, 2012).

[23] Besides these arrangements, Russia started to deliver oil to China by rail, under a contract concluded in 2005.

[24] Marcin Kaczmarski, *An Asian Alternative? Russia's Chances of making Asia an alternative to relations with the West*, Warsaw: Publisher Centre for Eastern Studies, June 2008, p. 48–51, http://www.osw.waw.pl/sites/default/files/PUNKT_WIDZENIA_16.pdf (February 2, 2012).

[25] Marcin Kaczmarski, Wojciech Konończuk, *The Russian-Chinese energy deal a sign of a new model of bilateral relations*, December 29, 2008, Centre for Eastern Studies, http://www.osw.waw.pl/en/publikacje/eastweek/2008-10-30/russian-chinese-energy-deal-sign-new-model-bilateral-relations (February 2, 2012).

Dwivedi Ramakant, "China's Central Asia Policy In Recent Times," *The China and Eurasia Forum Quarterly*, Central Asia-Caucasus Institute, Silk Road Studies Program, Vol. 4, No. 4, 2006.

Gacek Łukasz, "Oil In Chinese Foreign Policy," in: *Acta Asiatica Varsoviensia*, ed. by Roman M. Sławiński, No. 22, Polish Academy of Science, Centre for Studies on Non-European Countries, 2009.

Haliżak Edward, *Polityka i strategia Chin w kształtowaniu międzynarodowego bezpieczeństwa*, Żurawia Papers, Issue 10, Warszawa: Wydawnictwo Naukowe Scholar, 2007.

Jarosiewicz Aleksandra, *The Turkmenistan-China gas Pipeline Considerably Strengthens China's Position in Central Asia*, December 16, 2009, Centre for Eastern Studies, http://www.osw.waw.pl/en/publikacje/eastweek/2009-12-16/turkmenistan-china-gas-pipeline-considerably-strengthens-chinas-posit (February 2, 2012).

Jaroszewicz Aleksandra, Falkowski Maciej, *The Great Game around Turkmenistan*, Warsaw: Publisher Centre for Eastern Studies, August 2008, http://www.osw.waw.pl/sites/default/files/punkt_widzenia_17.pdf (February 2, 2012).

Jiang Wenran, "China Makes Strides in Energy 'Go-out' Strategy," *China Brief*, The Jamestown Foundation, Vol. 9, Issue 15, July 23, 2009, http://www.jamestown.org/programs/chinabrief/single/?tx_ttnews[tt_news]=35309&tx_ttnews[backPid]=25&cHash=1828d2cfe2 (February 2, 2012).

Kaczmarski Marcin, *An Asian Alternative? Russia's Chances of making Asia an alternative to relations with the West*, Warsaw: Publisher Centre for Eastern Studies, June 2008, http://www.osw.waw.pl/sites/default/files/PUNKT_WIDZENIA_16.pdf (February 2, 2012).

Kaczmarski Marcin, Konończuk Wojciech, *The Russian-Chinese Energy Deal a Sign of a New Model of Bilateral Relations*, December 29, 2008, Centre for Eastern Studies, http://www.osw.waw.pl/en/publikacje/eastweek/2008-10-30/russian-chinese-energy-deal-sign-new-model-bilateral-relations (February 2, 2012).

Kazakhstan Completes Oil Pipeline to China, July 14, 2009, Centre for Eastern Studies, http://www.osw.waw.pl/en/publikacje/eastweek/2009-07-15/kazakhstan-completes-oil-pipeline-china (February 2, 2012).

Lai Hongyi, "China Builds Bridges to Fuel Its Engine Room," *Financial Times*, July 4, 2010.

Peyrouse Sébastien, "Central Asia's Growing Partnership with China," *EUCAM Working Paper*, EUCAM EU-Central Asia Monitoring, No. 4, October 2009.

Peyrouse Sébastien, "Sino-Kazakh Relations: A Nascent Strategic Partnership," *China Brief*, The Jamestown Foundation, Vol. 8, Issue 21, November 4, 2008, http://www.jamestown.org/single/?no_cache=1&tx_ttnews[tt_news]=34142 (February 2, 2012).

U.S. Energy Information Administration, http://www.eia.gov/emeu/cabs/Kazakhstan/pdf.pdf (March 19, 2012).

Rosner Kevin, "China Scores Again in Energy: Russia & Central Asia," *Journal of Energy Security*, January 12, 2010, http://www.ensec.org/index.

php?option=com_content&view=article&id=230:china-scores-again-in-energy-russia-aamp-central-asia&catid=102:issuecontent&Itemid=355 (February 2, 2012).

Seaman John, *Energy Security, Transnational Pipelines and China's Role in Asia,* IFRI Centre Asie, April 2010.

Swanström Niklas, "China's Role In Central Asia: Soft and Hard Power," *Global Dialogue*, Vol. 9, No. 1–2, Winter–Spring 2007.

U.S. Energy Information Administration, http://www.eia.gov/countries/cab.cfm?fips=CH (March 19, 2012).

Wan Zhihong, "China, Kazakhstan Sign New Gas Pipeline Deal," *China Daily*, June 14, 2010.

Zapaśnik Stanisław, *Stosunki Chin z republikami Azji Centralnej*, in: *Azja Wschodnia na przełomie XX i XXI w.*, Vol. 2, *Stosunki międzynarodowe i gospodarcze*, ed. by Krzysztof Gawlikowski, Małgorzata Ławacz, ISP PAN, Warszawa: Wydawnictwo TRIO, 2004.

Chapter Eight

Karol Bronicki

Sino-Japanese Dispute over the Seabed Oil and Gas Resources in the East China Sea

East China Sea, together with the Yellow Sea and the South China Sea, is one of the three half-closed water basins, separating continental China from the Pacific Ocean. It is separated from the Pacific Ocean by the Ryukyu Archipelago; the Strait of Taiwan separates it from the South China Sea. To the north, it joins with the Yellow Sea, and through the Korean Strait, with the Sea of Japan. At its shores lie the three provinces of continental China: Fujian, Zhejiang and Jiangsu.[1] For many centuries it has been an important fishing area for its coastal countries, and is still important in terms of food security.

Between 1969 and 1970, rich oil and gas deposits of the East China Sea became a subject of interests of the countries lying at its shores. The claims were staked out by Japan, Okinawa (at that time being under the US administration), South Korea, and Taiwan. The unilateral claims were based on the Convention on the Continental Shelf, signed in Geneva in 1958,[2] and they referred to 11 seabed petroleum blocks altogether. The four Japanese blocks and Okinawa's block were claimed by private oil interests, unlike South Korea's two and Taiwan's four which were claimed by the respective governments.[3] Unilateral claims of Japan were supported by the so-called median principle, while Korea and Taiwan based on the natural prolongation of the shoreline principle. Inevitably, the claims

[1] Jan Rowiński, *Morze Wschodniochińskie – region potencjalnego konfliktu w Azji*, Warszawa: PISM, 1990, p. 2.

[2] However, Japan ignored the principle mentioned in the convention, that the continental shelf reaches only to the depth of 200 meters. Okinawa Trough, being deeper than that, would be considered as the end of Japanese continental shelf, and an obstacle to its claims.

[3] Choon-Ho Park, *Seabed Boundary Issues o the East China Sea*, http://www.wilsoncenter.org/topics/docs/Choon-Ho_Park_1_.pdf, p. 1 (January 29, 2012).

overlapped one another to different extents.[4] The dispute was partially solved in 1970, when the parties decided to reach an agreement on joined development of the resources. Due to PRC's strong protest, Taiwan withdrew from the talks. Korea and Japan proceeded with the scheme. The agreement, signed in 1974, consisted of two documents: one on the shelf boundary issue, and the second one (with mandatory period of 50 years, valid until 2028)[5] relating to joint development. The conflict, however, has not come to an end, as in the year of 1982, a new United Nations Convention on the Law of the Sea (UNCLOS) emerged, giving the disputing parties new legal possibilities to support their claims. Moreover, dynamic development caused China's demand for energy to rise immensely, even though in the beginning it were political reasons that drove this country into the dispute. Currently, however, China, dependent on resources imported mainly from the unstable Middle East region, cannot afford any breaks in the energy import supply, which could lead to economic crash, and social unrest as a consequence.[6] Exploration of the East China Sea and the Tarim Basin in Xinjiang province became the energy security priorities.[7] This explains how crucial it is for this country to have the East China Sea delimitation problems solved on their benefit. The East China Sea oil and gas deposits are important also to Japan, whose economy is highly dependent on resource import. As a result, the problem remains unsolved for already 40 years.

The continental shelf dispute and the Diaoyu/Senkaku Islands ownership issue

The size of the East China Sea basin is significant, although its exact scope is a matter of discussion. Western sources usually estimate about 300,000 square kilometers, or 162,000 square nautical miles. According to Chinese sources, however, the basin reaches 700,000 square kilometers, or 415,766 square nautical miles. The waters are shallow, with maximum depth not

[4] *Ibid.*

[5] *Ibid.*, p. 3.

[6] Arthur S. Ding, "China's Energy and Security Demands. A Growing Likehood of Conflict in East Asia?," *The China and Eurasia Forum Quarterly*, November 2005, p. 36–38, http://www.silkroadstudies.org/new/docs/CEF/Quarterly/November_2005/Arthur_Ding.pdf (January 29, 2012).

[7] James Manicom, *What is the East China Sea Worth? Conceptions of Value in Maritime Territorial Disputes*, Australasian Political Studies Association (APSA) Annual Conference, Monash University, September 24–26, 2007, p. 12, http://arts.monash.edu.au/psi/news-and-events/apsa/refereed-papers/international-relations/manicom.pdf (January 29, 2012).

reaching 200 meters (except for the Okinawa Trough, running alongside the Japanese Ryukyu archipelago). The seabed slopes gently from the Chinese coast until it drops abruptly into the Okinawa Trough (which the Chinese call Sino-Ryukyu Trough) whose depth reaches 2,300 meters at its deepest.[8] The Chinese doctrine claims that the Okinawa Trough proves a discontinuity between the continental shelf of China and Japan, with the trough as a natural demarcation between them. A support for this position can be found in the International Court of Justice's (ICJ) ruling in the case Libya vs. Malta (June 3, 1985), which stated that if there is a discontinuity between the continental shelf of two parties, the boundary should lie along the general line of this discontinuity.[9]

According to the UNCLOS, countries have the right to develop resources from the natural prolongation of their continental shelf. Article 76(1) defines a continental shelf as follows: "The continental shelf of a coastal State comprises the seabed and subsoil of the submarine areas that extend beyond its territorial sea throughout the natural prolongation of its land territory to the outer edge of the continental margin, or to a distance of 200 nautical miles from the baselines from which the breadth of the territorial sea is measured where the outer edge of the continental margin does not extend up to that distance." Article 76(6) however states that "(...) on submarine ridges, the outer limit of the continental shelf shall not exceed 350 nautical miles from the baselines from which the breadth of the territorial sea is measured (...)."[10]

China refers to those articles and states that the East China Sea is a natural prolongation of the continental territory of China, which has inviolable sovereignty over its continental shelf. As some scholars point out, Chinese claims, extending on the whole of the continental shelf to the Okinawa Trough, that is 350 nautical miles from the coast of China, cover all of the potential seabed oil and gas resources in the East China Sea. The problem for Chinese argumentation might be posed by the Diaoyudao Uplift Belt, which raises the continental shelf, resembling a 'w' shape. This geological form might be used as a proof of East China Sea basin continental shelf discontinuity, which would work against Chinese right to the whole of the continental shelf, and likely to a large part of the oil and gas deposits located around the islands, especially, if the Japanese

[8] James C. Hsiung, *Sea Power, Law of the Sea and China-Japan "Resource War,"* Forum on China and the Sea, Institute of Sustainable Development, Macao University of Science & Technology, Macao, China, October 9–11, 2005, p. 5–6, http://www.nyu.edu/gsas/dept/politics/faculty/hsiung/sea_power.pdf (January 29, 2012).

[9] *Ibid.*, p. 6.

[10] *United Nations Convention on the Law of the Sea*, December 10, 1982, 1833 U.N.T.S. 397, http://www.un.org/Depts/los/convention_agreements/texts/unclos/closindx.htm (January 29, 2012).

side can prove the right to the Senkaku/Diaoyu to their own continental shelf. Their position may find support in the mentioned ICJ ruling (Libya vs. Malta), as it proved that entitlement for the continental shelf is the same for islands and a continental state.[11]

Another UNCLOS rule which may be applied in the matter is the one concerning Exclusive Economic Zones (EEZ). Article 57 of the UNCLOS states that an EEZ cannot exceed over 200 nautical miles from the baselines, from which the territorial sea is measured. Japan and China are two states with opposite coasts, but the body of waters between them is less than 400 nautical miles in total. The width varies from 180 nautical miles at the narrowest points to 360 nautical miles at the widest. It is 1,300 kilometers (or 702 nautical miles) in length from north to south.[12] Presence of two EEZs in the zone might pose serious conflicts. Theoretically, a solution to this problem lies in the article 74(1) of the UNCLOS: "The delimitation of the exclusive economic zone between States with opposite or adjacent coasts shall be effected by agreement on the basis of international law, as referred to in Article 38 of the Statute of the International Court of Justice, in order to achieve an equitable solution." It is worth mentioning that the article 74(1) does not only refer to the international law, but also directly to article 38 of the ICJ statute, which says that despite the conventions the court applies also "international custom, as evidence of a general practice accepted as law" and "the general principles of law recognized by civilized nations."[13] The specific wording in article 74(1) of the LOS Convention, therefore, is so chosen as to drive home that in arriving at a mutual agreement regarding delimitation of their EEZ boundaries, the opposite states should take a wider consideration of all facts and norms within the context of general international law, thus defined, which is larger than the law of the sea *per se*.[14] Due to the lack of an agreement between the parties whatsoever, Japan unilaterally drew a "median line" to demarcate the EEZs. The following line not only does exceed beyond what is a line consistent of points equidistant from the coastal baselines of the two countries, but also makes a turn to the west to enclose the disputed Senkaku/Diaoyu islands in the Japanese EEZ. The islets, controlled by Japan since the 19th century, lie between 25°42' latitude North and between 123°25' and 123°26' longitude East, 380 kilometers north-east of Taiwan, and a similar distance north of the Japanese Sakishima islands.[15]

[11] Alexander M. Peterson, "Sino-Japanese Cooperation in the East China Sea: A Lasting Agreement?," 42 *Cornell International Law Journal*, February 24, 2010, p. 455–456.

[12] Hsiung, *op. cit.*, p. 6.

[13] *Statute of the International Court of Justice*, http://www.icj-cij.org/documents/index.php?p1=4&p2=2&p3=0 (January 29, 2012).

[14] Hsiung, *op. cit.*, p. 6–7.

[15] Rowiński, *op. cit.*, p. 6.

Until 1971, the islets remained under US administration, and were treated as a part of the Ryukyu archipelago. The following status of the Senkaku/Diaoyu was caused by strategic matters. The command of the American forces in that area had a special interest in this state of affairs, as the islets were included into Ryukyu defense system. The islets were *de facto* considered by the USA as a part of Japanese territory. For instance, the US Navy paid an annual rent of 11 thousands dollars to the son of the first Japanese settler of the Diaoyu Islands as compensation for its use of one of the islands as a firing range, which continued until 1978.[16] As the Ryukyu were passed to Japan, the United States distanced themselves from any judgments concerning sovereignty over the islands, claiming that it was a question to be regulated by the two countries themselves. It appears, however, that the United States should be more involved in the solution of the dispute, as the lack of their official position on that matter poses questions whether the Japanese-American alliance treaty of 1960 applies also to the disputed islands. The United States might thus be forced to support one of the parties' positions in the future.[17] The Diaoyu/Senkaku dispute, taking place already since 1970, might seem an absurd at first glance. The archipelago consists of eight small and uninhabited islets, which are hardly visible on most maps and do not have any sources of drinkable water. However, they are surrounded by significant oil and gas deposits. They also have a strategic meaning, as they lie on the route of important sea lines of communication (SLOCs), and give a possibility to build military installations, such as helipads or VTOL aircraft pads, radars, or even construction of artificial islands with such installations. Part of the scholars claim that, to a great extent, the dispute is caused by symbolic value of the islands, or it is just another instrument of Chinese pressure.[18]

Japan considers all the waters on the eastern side of its „median line" as an area of its exclusive jurisdiction. The Chinese side states that such a line should run in the middle of the distance between the western coast of Japanese Ryukyu islands, and the eastern coast of Taiwan, which Beijing considers as a part of PR China's territory. If the median line was drawn this way, even without including Taiwan, the Diaoyu Islands would be lying in the Chinese EEZ, which would be unacceptable for Tokyo.

Since the 1970s, China has been claiming sovereign rights over Diaoyutai by raising mostly historical arguments,[19] mainly prior discovery

[16] Jean-Marc F. Blanchard, "The US Role in the Sino-Japanese Dispute over Diaoyu (Senkaku) Islands," *The China Quarterly*, No. 161, March 2000, p. 97.

[17] *Ibid.*, p. 120–121.

[18] *Ibid.*, p. 122.

[19] See: Miyoshi Masahiro, *Seabed Petroleum of the East China Sea: Law of the Sea Issues and Prospects for Joint Development*, Faculty of Law, Aichi University, Japan, p. 3–5, http://www.wilsoncenter.org/topics/docs/Miyoshi_Masahiro.pdf (January 29, 2012); Rowiński, *op. cit.*, p. 11–13.

and use of the islands. The Chinese stood firmly on the position that the archipelago was annexed by Japan under the Treaty of Shimonoseki signed in 1985, as a part of Taiwan's surrounding islands mentioned in the treaty. The Japanese arguments are mostly based on modern rules of the Law of the Sea, and the fact that they have had sustainable control of the islands even before the Chinese staked out their claims. Also in this case, according to most specialists, it is Japan who has superiority in legal arguments for supporting their cause. Firstly, it is unlikely that the Chinese will be able to prove a connection between the treaty of Shimonoseki and the islands, as they were not literarily mentioned in the document. Secondly, there is an ICJ ruling to support Japanese claims, namely the Pulau Ligitan and Pulau Sipadan case (Indonesia vs. Malaysia), which showed that effective control (seen as occupation and rapid protest against foreign encroachments) supersedes the historical title in terms of island sovereignty.[20]

Another problem is whether the Senkaku/Diaoyu are or are not eligible for having their own continental shelf. Article 121(3) of the UNCLOS reads as follows: „Rocks which cannot sustain human habitation or economic life of their own shall have no exclusive economic zone or continental shelf."[21] China claims that the Senkaku/Diaoyu, being small, uninhabitable, and not able to sustain economic activity on its own, should not be the base point for any claims of the EEZ or continental shelf. Japanese standpoint is quite the opposite. According to Tokyo, this territory should be treated as fully fledged islands, and thus have the right to their own continental shelf and economic zone. Basing on this statement, they treat the islands as the base point for their claims on the East China Sea. In the mentioned issue, only one thing is certain. The Senkaku/Diaoyu has by now resisted any legal or pragmatic solutions, since it is dependent on the parties' internal affairs.[22]

[20] Peterson, *Sino-Japanese...*, p. 451–453.

[21] *United Nations Convention on the Law of the Sea...*

[22] James Manicom, in his article "What is the East China Sea Worth? Conceptions of value in maritime territorial disputes," points out the high level of involvement in the dispute of both countries' nationalist movements. As an example, he brings forward the Japanese rightist politician Nishimura Singo's landing on the Diaoyu in 1997, and similar attempts of nationalist organizations from Hong Kong and Taiwan. As the most important groups of actors influencing the conflict management inside both parties, he mentions the core policymakers (governments), peripheral policymakers (for example Nishimura's party), and nationalist lobby groups, such as Japanese *Nihon Seinensha*, or the mainland Chinese *China Federation for Defending Diaoyu*. Manicom, *op. cit.*, p. 2–8.

Dispute at its latest stage: obstacles and steps towards cooperation

The UNCLOS came into force on 14th November 1994; one year after it was signed by the sixtieth state.[23] In accordance with this convention, Japan declared its EEZ in 1996, and China in 1998. Despite the lack of any delimitation agreement, the Chinese started geological researches in the 1980s in order to develop the resources of the so-called Xihu Trough, which lies less than 200 nautical miles (370.4 km) from the nearest point of Chinese coastal baselines, or 215 nautical miles (398 km) in a straight line from the Chinese port of Ningbo in the north-east. Natural gas deposits of the area are estimated at 300 billion cubic feet. The Chinese planned to establish seven natural gas and oil fields in total, including Pinghu, Canxue, Duanqiao, Tianwaitian, and Chunxiao sites, with the total area of 22,000 square kilometers (11,879 nautical miles).[24] Pinghu site, lying on an undisputed area, started functioning already in 1998, with the gas being transported to Shanghai via underwater pipelines.

National Oceanic Bureau in Beijing, inquired about the precise distance between the Xihu Trough and the Chinese coast, belittled these concerns by claiming their little significance due to the fact that the whole area lies on the Chinese continental shelf. Some of the specialists, such as James C. Hsiung of the New York University, do not agree with this point, claiming that the significance of this question cannot be underestimated. If the Xihu Trough lied closer than 200 nautical miles from the Chinese baselines, the Chinese rights for development of it as a part of their EEZ would be out of discussion, even considering Japanese boundary claims. According to article 56 of the UNCLOS, in their EEZ, China would have „sovereign rights for the purpose of exploring and exploiting, conserving and managing the natural resources (...), of the waters superjacent to the seabed and its subsoil."[25]

In 2003, the Chinese National Offshore Oil Company (CNOOC) and the China Petroleum & Chemical Corporation (Sinopec) entered into a joint venture agreement with Unocal (the 8th largest oil company in the USA) and the Royal Dutch/Shell for oil development. The two foreign partners withdrew from the agreement in 2004,[26] and the Chinese proceeded on their own, starting the drillings in 2005.

[23] Peterson, *Exploration of the East China Sea: The Law of the Sea in Practice*, Bepress Legal Series, Working Paper 1730, p. 3.

[24] Hsiung, *op. cit.*, p. 7.

[25] *United Nations Convention on the Law of the Sea...*

[26] Xie Ye, „Oil Giants pull out of East China Sea," *China Daily*, September 30, 2004, http://www.chinadaily.com.cn/english/doc/2004-09/30/content_379072.htm (January 29, 2012).

Most of the Xihu Trough (about 80 percent) lies on the Chinese side of the Japanese 'median line.' Probably, the most important oil field in this area is the Chunxiao, which lies about 150 miles from the Chinese coast, and about 5 kilometers west from the Japanese 'median line,' which proves undoubtedly, even considering Japanese claims, that it lies in the Chinese EEZ. Nevertheless, Japan protested strongly against the drillings, which, according to the Japanese, posed a threat of siphoning the part of oil and gas deposits that lies in the Japanese EEZ.

The location of Chunxiao field in the undisputed zone might have been chosen on purpose in order to avoid conflict escalation. This was also an aim for Japanese policy, considering that for a long time, Tokyo has sustained a ban on East China Sea exploration by Japanese companies. However, as a result of Chinese drillings, the ban was lifted in 2005, as the Japanese government expressed readiness to accept companies' applications for East China Sea development licenses. According to Japanese press releases, two companies, Japanese Exploration Co. and Teikoku Oil Co. (which renewed its exploration applications put forward in the 1960s), were looking for government approval to explore resources in the area placed about 450 km (243 nautical miles) west of Okinawa, at least 43 miles behind the Japanese EEZ, within the Chinese maritime territory.[27] After the Japanese ban was lifted, Teikoku was granted the license even sooner than expected, on 14th July 2005.[28] It became the source of heavy tensions in Sino-Japanese relations, and caused an immediate reaction of the Chinese foreign ministry. Subsequently, a strong wave of government-inspired anti-Japanese protests took place in the whole country.[29] In addition, Chinese fleet and air force were put into the state of emergency in case of any violation of Chinese sovereign rights by the Japanese oil companies. In September 2005, the conflict reached its escalation when five Chinese warships, including a Sovremenny class missile destroyer, were spotted in a close distance from the Chunxiao field. One of the warships took aim on a Japanese P3-C reconnaissance aircraft patrolling the area.[30] The parties decided that the tensions should be solved by bilateral negotiations. A day before the actual beginning of the planned talks, however, China confirmed sending a reserve fleet detachment to the East China Sea, which was capable of carrying out wartime operations and elimination of sea obstacles.

---

[27] Hsiung, *op. cit.*, p. 8.

[28] Mayumi Negishi, "Teikoku Oil Gets Drilling Rights in East China Sea," *The Japan Times*, July 15, 2005, http://www.japantimes.co.jp/text/nn20050715a1.html (January 29, 2012).

[29] See: Manicom, *op. cit.*, p. 14–15; Peterson, *Sino-Japanese...*, p. 458–459.

[30] Ding, *op. cit.*, p. 35.

Japan considered this act, together with the detection of a Chinese nuclear submarine on Japanese territorial waters in November 2004, enlarged activity of electronic reconnaissance by the Chinese air force, and encroachment of about 25 Chinese exploration vessels into Japanese waters during the last 6 months, as a potential threat from the Chinese side. In their security and defense plan, the Japanese Defense Forces for the first time mentioned China as a potential threat, and suggested several possible scenarios, including a brigade-sized invasion on the Senkaku/Diaoyu islands. The Chinese protest against East China Sea penetration was reduced to a statement that the sovereign territory of China was violated. However, it did not specify from which point in terms of geographical coordinates will Japanese activity be considered as a violation of theChinese territory.[31]

Tokyo's decision to lift the East China Sea exploration ban mentioned before was probably inspired by the reaction of Japanese society to the information about the Chinese Chunxiao field being ready to start the drillings until October 2005. After finishing the construction works, the Chunxiao field was estimated to provide approximately 2.5 thousand cubic meters of gas per year to the Shanghai region via an underwater pipeline network. The Japanese unrest caused by that matter was explained very clearly and graphically by Japanese minister of trade, Shoichi Nakagawa. Confronting a Chinese negotiator face to face, Nakagawa dramatically dropped two straws in a glass of orange juice, and foregoing all Japanese customary politeness complained that China was about to „suck out Japan's resources with a straw."[32] As he claimed, which was proved by the latest seismic ship survey found, two oil deposits that were to be developed by China, including Chunxiao, extend to the Japanese EEZ. Regardless of this issue, one thing is certain: the 'sucking straw' problem showed by Nakagawa cannot be solved by neither UNCLOS nor modern law of the sea.

Many specialists, such as Jeffrey Kingston, an American expert in Japanese affairs, argue that the EEZ delimitation problem is just a small part of an enormous gap between Japan and China in terms of their mutual relations, and they cannot be solved simply by rules of law or even pure pragmatics. This would explain why a conjoint development offer was rejected by Japan during the fourth round of negotiation talks in 2006, and a Japanese request for information on Chinese East China Sea exploration did not meet with a positive answer from Beijing.[33] The negotiations were even prolonged, as the Japanese Prime Minister Junichiro

[31] ISN Security Watch, http://www.isn.ethz.ch/ (June 28, 2012).

[32] Hsiung, *op. cit.*, p. 9.

[33] Peterson, *Exploration*..., p. 28.

Koizumi made anti-Chinese actions a part of his policy. Nevertheless, 11 rounds of negotiation talks were held between 2004 and 2008. Koizumi's successor, Shinzo Abe, made efforts to improve the bilateral relations by hosting Chinese Prime Minister Wen Jiabao in Tokyo in 2007. Even though no important decisions were made, the meeting evoked a positive atmosphere between the parties. Even though Abe's administration lasted only for one year, his successor, Yasuo Fukuda, continued the Sino-Japanese warm-up policy. The positive trend gave a significant boost to the East China Sea negotiation talks, which resulted in a joint development agreement on 18th June 2008. The declaration had a form of a mutual announcement of foreign ministry representatives of both parties, and sought to make the East China Sea a "sea of peace, cooperation and friendship." Furthermore, 2,700 square kilometers of East China Sea area were to be jointly explored by Japan and China, and Japanese corporations were to invest in the Chunxiao field. Later on, the Chinese side had to calm its public opinion and domestic criticism by clarifying that the agreement did not imply conjoint development of the Chunxiao, which was undisputedly Chinese. The agreement was, however, threatened between late 2008 and 2010 by strongly nationalistic and anti-Chinese policy of the new Japanese prime minister Taro Aso, who was later succeeded by Yukio Hatoyama. Until today, in spite of many obstacles, the agreement has been sustained. However, it has not yet brought any measurable results. Moreover, specialists argue that the agreement is not legally binding, which means that neither of the parties would meet any legal consequences in case of withdrawal. It should thus be seen more as a significant, but not decisive step into further cooperation.[34]

Miyoshi Masahiro of the Japanese Aichi University's Faculty of Law believes that this problem is likely to be finally solved in a conjoint development agreement, giving an example of such agreements with South Korea and other similar regulations which took place in the past.[35] Moreover, Japan and China have already had experience in cooperative development of resources.[36] The matter, however, instead of being solved, is regularly being escalated by one side or the other. It has been done ever since the disputes began, only to mention an armed excursion of Chinese 'fishing fleet' to the Diaoyu islands area in April 1978, construction of a lighthouse on one of the islets by Japanese nationalists in 1978, declaration of official registration of this lighthouse by Japanese Maritime Security Agency in 1990, construction of another lighthouse by Japanese

[34] See: Peterson, *Sino-Japanese...*, p. 457–473.

[35] See: Masahiro, *op. cit.*, p. 5–12.

[36] See: Peterson, *Exploration...*, p. 24–26.

nationalists in 1996, or hacking attacks on Japanese websites of 2004.[37] There is another reason why a purely legal solution to the conflict is difficult. As many researchers believe, international legal practice and precedent speaks in favor of Japan.[38]. Any ruling by an international court unfavorable to China would make the rising power lose its face, as it would have to withdraw from its present negotiation points or clearly break international law. The situation would be similar in the case of Japan, if at some point the country was forced to withdraw under the Chinese pressure. Some sort of an agreement as a solution to the conflict would definitely be the most beneficial for the both parties. However, considering the current level of animosities between them, it is not as simple as it would appear.

Second row participants

Despite the fact that the two most important players in the East China Sea dispute are the People's Republic of China and Japan, the position of the other two actors, Republic of Korea and Taiwan, is also worth to be mentioned. Taiwan, analogically as the People's Republic of China, claims sovereignty over Senkaku/Diaoyu, and states that they do not have any right to its own continental shelf or Exclusive Economic Zone whatsoever, and thus they should not have any impact on East China Sea boundary issues. South Korea, similarly to China, stands on position that the presence of Okinawa Trough in the East China Sea basin creates special circumstances, which exclude application of the median line principle. All of the disputing parties have the right to claim 200 miles of their own EEZ, but the delimitation issue was raised by Korea and Japan in the first place, as both countries declared their EEZ's in February 1996. Japan, Korea, and Taiwan have all been claiming 200 nautical miles of their own EEZ basing on the UNCLOS. South Korea stands on position that wherever the economic zones overpass each other, the delimitation issues should be solved by mutual agreements between the states. Considering the fact that all of the parties (except for Taiwan) signed the UNCLOS, the delimitation issues should not pose any problems. The problems, however, do exist, and they seem to be significant. The states disagree even on such basic issues as which party has the sovereignty over a certain territory, or whether certain parts of it can or cannot be taken

[37] "Organized Chinese hackers Hit Official Japan Sites," Kyodo, *The Japan Times*, August 7, 2004, http://www.japantimes.co.jp/text/nn20040807a3.html (January 29, 2012).

[38] See: Peterson, *Exploration...*, p. 20–23.

as the base points for delimitation. Until this day, Korea and Japan cannot reach an agreement on their EEZ boundary issues. Japan, a sovereign over the Danjo Gunto islands, declares the boundary between Japanese and Korean EEZs to run in equidistance between the Danjo Gunto and the coast of Korea. South Korea does not deny Japanese sovereignty over the islands; however, Seoul claims that the islands lie on Korean continental shelf, and thus do not provide the base point for EEZ claims. The situation is parallel to the Sino-Japanese Diaoyu/Senkaku dispute, with exception that Korea and Japan were able to reach an agreement on conjoint development in the area.

Conclusion

A solution to Sino-Japanese issues seems to be difficult to reach at the present time, as none of the parties is driven only by pragmatics and will for an agreement. A possible solution by cooperation would bring the parties significant benefits to both parties. Firstly, they would both avoid a loss of face because none would have to officially admit defeat. In addition, China would be able to obtain high technologies which they need for effective development of resources. Japan, as one of the most important investors in China, would have its business secured, and Chinese market likely opened for further expansion, not to mention the possibility of increased tourist movement between the states. An agreement would also show them as responsible powers able to peacefully resolve important problems between them. Even though cooperation would seem a perfect win-win solution, the dispute remains a crossing point for both Chinese and Japanese crucial strategic goals and aspirations. Cooperation is especially difficult as the actors still have not dealt with their difficult relations in the history, and cannot overlook their public opinions. If the conflict continues to be managed as roughly as it used to be in the past, and the parties' negotiation points remain unchanged, we might observe an escalation of the conflict in the near future. All of the mentioned conflicts can be seen as an emanation of increased regional struggle for sea domination.

Bibliography

Blanchard Jean-Marc F., “The US Role in the Sino-Japanese Dispute over Diaoyu (Senkaku) Islands,” *The China Quarterly*, No. 161, March 2000.

Choon-Ho Park, *Seabed Boundary Issues o the East China Sea*, http://www.wilsoncenter.org/topics/docs/Choon-Ho_Park_1_.pdf (January 29, 2012).

Ding Arthur S., “China’s Energy and Security Demands. A Growing Likehood of Conflict in East Asia?,” *The China and Eurasia Forum Quarterly*, November 2005, http://www.silkroadstudies.org/new/docs/CEF/Quarterly/November_2005/Arthur_Ding.pdf (January 29, 2012).

Hsiung James C., *Sea Power, Law of the Sea and China-Japan “Resource War,”* Forum on China and the Sea, Institute of Sustainable Development, Macao University of Science & Technology, Macao, China, October 9–11, 2005, http://www.nyu.edu/gsas/dept/politics/faculty/hsiung/sea_power.pdf (January 29, 2012).

ISN Security Watch, http://www.isn.ethz.ch/ (June 28, 2012).

Manicom James, *What is the East China Sea Worth? Conceptions of Value in Maritime Territorial Disputes*, Australasian Political Studies Association (APSA) Annual Conference, Monash University, September 24–26, 2007, http://arts.monash.edu.au/psi/news-and-events/apsa/refereed-papers/international-relations/manicom.pdf (January 29, 2012).

Masahiro Miyoshi, *Seabed Petroleum of the East China Sea: Law of the Sea Issues and Prospects for Joint Development*, Faculty of Law, Aichi University, Japan, http://www.wilsoncenter.org/topics/docs/Miyoshi_Masahiro.pdf (January 29, 2012).

Negishi Mayumi, “Teikoku Oil gets drilling rights in East China Sea,” *The Japan Times*, July 15, 2005, http://www.japantimes.co.jp/text/nn20050715a1.html (January 29, 2012).

“Organized Chinese Hackers Hit Official Japan Sites,” Kyodo, *The Japan Times*, August 7, 2004, http://www.japantimes.co.jp/text/nn20040807a3.html (January 29, 2012).

Peterson Alexander M., *Exploration of the East China Sea: The Law of the Sea in Practice*, Bepress Legal Series, Working Paper, 1730.

Peterson Alexander M., “Sino-Japanese Cooperation in the East China Sea: A Lasting Agreement?,” *42 Cornell International Law Journal*, February 24, 2010.

Rowiński Jan, *Morze Wschodniochińskie – region potencjalnego konfliktu w Azji*, Warszawa: PISM, 1990.

Statute of the International Court of Justice, http://www.icj-cij.org/documents/index.php?p1=4&p2=2&p3=0 (January 29, 2012).

United Nations Convention on the Law of the Sea, December 10, 1982, 1833 U.N.T.S. 397, http://www.un.org/Depts/los/convention_agreements/texts/unclos/closindx.htm (January 29, 2012).

Ye Xie, „Oil Giants pull out of East China Sea,” *China Daily*, September 30, 2004, http://www.chinadaily.com.cn/english/doc/2004-09/30/content_379072.htm (January 29, 2012).

Chapter Nine

Jacek Budziaszek

China's Territorial Disputes in the South China Sea

The disputable area

When discussing the issue of territorial claims in the South China Sea, one should take the conglomerate of diverse phenomena influencing the specifics of thereof into account. The acts of aggression observed among some participants of the dispute, the growing global importance of China, and the contest for fossil fuels are only some of the problems expected to play extraordinarily important roles here. Any potential dispute of a military character in the region would undoubtedly have an overpowering influence on global economy, and would lead to disturbance of the current geopolitical balance. The specific role played by China in the East Asia makes all territorial claims being often considered in the context of the so-called 'Chinese threat,' contributing to the growth of apprehensions among the neighboring countries. The struggle for access to natural resources, however, seems to constitute the crucial field of conflict in the South China Sea area. International provisions on maritime borders do not specify the dependency of certain territories which additionally complicates the problem.

The South China Sea is a waterbody of total area of 3 537 000 km^2. In its northwestern part, in the distance of only ca. 300 km to the south from the Chinese island Hainan and 250 km from the coast of Vietnam, lies the archipelago of Paracel Islands, the key subject of dispute between Beijing and Hanoi. The archipelago, spread over a significant area of 15 000 km^2, consists of over 30 islets, sandbanks, and coral reefs, is divided into two groups. The first, Amphitrite, comprises 8 islets and coral reefs, constituting the northeastern part of the archipelago. The biggest, and simultaneously the easternmost of them, the Lincoln Island (Chinese names:

Wuhe Dao or Dong Dao; Vietnamese name: Dao Linh Con; dimensions: 2.3/0.8 km^2), lies nearby a highly-congested seaway, connecting the Indian and the Pacific Ocean, which determines its importance. The second, western group of the Paracel Islands archipelago, named Crescent, consists of 7 isles, and numerous small coral reefs and sandbanks. The Spratly Islands (Chinese name: Nansha Qundao, Vietnamese name: Truong Sa), also known as the Coral Islands, is an archipelago, spread over an area of over 400 000 km^2 in the southeastern part of the South China Sea, ca. 400 km from the coast of the Philippines and 600 km from southern Vietnam. It consists of 160 topographic objects: islands, islets, rocky sandbanks, atolls, and reefs, some of which are submerged in the water. The biggest island of the Spratly archipelago is Itu Aba (dimensions: 0.6/4 km), belonging to the island group named Tizard Bank, located in the center of the archipelago. The other 11 groups of islands, starting from southwest, are: Amboyna Cay, Commodore Reef, Marveles Reef, Union Bank, Spratley, Irving Cay, Nanshan, Loaita, Thitu, North Danger, and West York Island.[1]

Historical argumentation of participants of the dispute

The key participants of the dispute, China and Vietnam, present numerous historical arguments referring to the issue of political status of Paracel and Spratly Islands archipelagos.[2] Many arguments are presented in centuries-old relics, including maps, documents or formal texts, like official correspondence, historical chronicles, and journey diaries. According to the Chinese, archeological research indicates the presence of representatives of the Han dynasty in the disputable area already in the 2nd century BC.[3]

The Vietnamese, on the other hand, refer to the period before the 17th century, claiming at the same time that their long-term supremacy over the Paracel Islands was only broken in result of the French invasion at the end of 19th century.[4] According to Edward Haliżak, in the period preced-

[1] See: Yann-huei Song, "United States and Territorial Disputes in the South China Sea: A study of Ocean Law and Politics," *Maryland Series In Contempropary Asian Studies*, No. 1 (168), School of Law University of Maryland, 2002, p. 18–24; Jan Rowiński, *Morze Południowochińskie – region potencjalnego konfliktu w Azji*, Warszawa: PISM, 1990, p. 19–27; *Atlas geograficzny świata*, ed. by Zofia Cukierka, Warszawa–Wrocław: Polskie Przedsiębiorstwo Wydawnictw Kartograficznych im. E. Romera, 1997, p. 132.

[2] The common history of the two countries makes the argumentation of Beijing and Taipei's authorities identical when referring to the period before 1950.

[3] Rowiński, *op. cit.*, p. 35.

[4] Saleem Omar, "The Spratly Islands Dispute: China Defines the New Millennium", *American University International Law Review* 15, No. 3 (2000), p. 541.

ing the French occupation of Indochina, the western publications used to regard the Paracel Islands as a part of the Kingdom of Vietnam, *inter alia* thanks to the presence of a Vietnamese Buddhist temple on one of the islands.[5] The old documents, referred to mostly by the Chinese, even if found authentic, remain almost meaningless in the context of the contemporarily binding international law. They mostly reflect the Chinese point of view, often contrary to the positions of other concerned parties. The Chinese provide a series of evidences from various historical periods, mostly from the few recent centuries, justifying their rights to this territory. According to Martin Stuart Fox, the naval campaigns from the times of Kublai Khan (late 13th century) should be regarded as the first signs of the power of Chinese navigation in the area of the South China Sea.[6]

The currently developed sea potential of China recalls these times. Other states participating in the dispute, such as the Philippines, Malaysia, and Brunei, do not refer to their histories so often. It does not, however, make a big difference as historical referrals, made mostly by China and Vietnam, are mostly of a symbolical character.

The participants of the dispute present their claims

International regulations on the continental shelf and exclusive economic zone (EEZ), included in the *Convention of the Law of the Sea*, establishes the basis for territorial claims of Vietnam, the Philippines, Malaysia, and Brunei. The *Convention*, binding since 1982, enables these states to control the islands and exploit natural resources located within the EEZ's borders or the continental shelf. A characteristic position is held by Beijing, since it prefers its domestic legal acts to the international law. Particular attention is brought by the *Territorial Sea Act*, adopted by the Chinese National People's Congress in February 1992, treating the majority of disputable areas as parts of Chinese territory, which is in direct contradiction to the provisions of the Law of the Sea.[7] Moreover, the *Declaration of the Government of the People's Republic of China*, published in 1996, defined China as the sole legal beneficiary of all natural resources in this area. In this context, international indignation was caused by the fact that the declaration assumed a practical end of free navigation in the waters of

[5] Edward Haliżak, *Spór o archipelagi na Morzu Południowochińskim. Historyczna debata i działania związane z przynależnością państwową Wysp Paracelskich i Spratley*, Warszawa, 2008, p. 177.

[6] Martin Stuart-Fox, *A Short History of China and Southeast Asia: Tribute, Trade and Influence*, London: A & U Press, 2003, p. 63.

[7] Haliżak, *op. cit.*, p. 180.

a crucial meaning for cargo transport. The People's Republic of China's (PRC) authorities, however, gave up on implementing this law. Another exemplification of a specific Chinese argumentation in legal issues was the attempt to provide the Paracel Islands with the status of an archipelago state under the provisions of the *Convention of the Law of the Sea*.[8]

In the first decade of the 20th century, during the rule of the last Chinese dynasty (Qing), some efforts were made to take control over the Paracel Islands. This may be proved by official communicates, aimed at confirming the dependence of the islands from China, as well as by dispatching warships of Chinese imperial navy to execute control mission.[9] In these difficult times, however, such actions were not effective due to the growing importance of colonial powers.

The first documents of international law, plainly and clearly identifying the archipelagos, were issued in the times when the French governor of Cochinchina declared the annexation of thereof, providing them with the official status of a part of the French Indochina. In the case of Spratley, it took place in 1933, while in case of Paracel Islands – eight years later.[10] Already in 1939 both archipelagos were occupied by the Japanese navy, taking advantage of their strategic localization during the invasion in Southeast Asia. Only after the Potsdam Conference in 1945, numerous islands were retaken from Japan, also including the archipelagos of Paracel and Spratley Islands.[11] Only a year afterwards, the troops of the Republic of China took over the non-occupied islands located in the northeast part of the Paracel archipelago. The victory of the Communists in the Chinese Civil War, and the evacuation of the Nationalists to Taiwan resulted in the beginning of operations of the Chinese People's Liberation Army's naval forces in the area of the mentioned islands in 1950. In mid 1950s, the northeast part of the Paracel Islands was already under Chinese control, while the islands in the southwest part of the archipelago fell under the control of South Vietnam after they were seized by the French troops.[12] The rivalry over the archipelagos in the South China Sea in the 1950s was to a large extent a derivative of the postwar tensions, resulting from the forming of the bipolar system of global powers, dominated by the United States and the Soviet Union. The unsolved problem of boundaries in the South China Sea became more important in mid 1960s when geological

8 Ralf Emmers, *Geopolitics and Maritime Territorial Disputes in East Asia*, London: Routledge, 2010, p. 71.

9 Rowiński, *op. cit.*, p. 38.

10 Christopher C. Joyner, "The Spratly Islands Dispute in the South China Sea: Problems, Policies, and Prospects for Diplomatic Accommodation," *New England Law Review*, Vol. 32, No. 3, 1998, p. 61.

11 Omar, *op. cit.*, p. 549.

12 Emmers, *op. cit.*, p. 68.

research evidenced the presence of huge resources of crude oil and natural gas in this area.[13] This fact encouraged China, Taiwan, and Vietnam (and later also the Philippines, Malaysia, and Brunei) to undertake intensive actions aimed at strengthening their positions in the battle for raw materials. It is worth mentioning that since the Chinese-Taiwan relations improved, the actions taken by the government in Taipei are rather limited to keeping the *status quo*, i.e. the control over the Itu Aba Island, occupied since 1956.[14] In 1971, the Taiwanese troops quartering there shelled Philippine fishermen working in the neighboring area. In result, the authorities in Manila officially submitted the claim for a group of islands in the Spratly archipelago.[15] Malaysia joined the dispute in 1978, submitting claims for twelve topographical objects in the southern part of the Spratley Islands. Half of them fell under constant control of this state in 2005. The last country to join the dispute in the 1980s was Brunei, supporting its claims by the international provisions resulting from the UNCLOS, and the argument of geographical proximity. The claims of the sultanate, however, are only restricted to the sea surrounding sandbanks near Spratly Islands and the Rifleman reefs. Therefore, the participation of Brunei in this conflict can be considered to be only of a partial character.[16]

So far, the states-participants of the dispute have usually tried to occupy part of the territory, and to install their troops there. Constant presence in the islands is important for the participants of the dispute for two reasons. Firstly, it allows for keeping actual control over the area surrounding them, partially located nearby raw material deposits. Secondly, in accordance with the binding international law, long-term occupation of islands, in some cases, may determine their final status.[17]

The evolution of the Chinese standpoint in this matter is one of the most interesting problems here. In the early 1970s, the PRC's troops made unsuccessful attempts at capturing the Duncan I and Robert Islands from the Crescent group, located in the southwest part of the Paracel archipelago. One of these attempts resulted in an encounter with the South Vietnam's navy ship in August 1973, and withdrawal of PRC's ships. On January 18th–20th 1974, PRC's navy executed another operation, which allowed it to defeat the Saigon forces, and, therefore, capture standing posts on both of the abovementioned islands.[18] The authorities of the so-

[13] Joyner, *op. cit.*, p. 58.

[14] Kristen Nordhaug, *Taiwan and the South China Sea Conflict: the China Connection Revisited*, Centre for Development and the Environment, Oslo, Norway, April, 1999, p. 48.

[15] Joyner, *op. cit.*, p. 61.

[16] Emmers, *op. cit.*, p. 69.

[17] Remigiusz Bierzanek, Janusz Symonides, *Prawo międzynarodowe publiczne*, Warszawa: Lexis Nexis, 2003.

[18] Haliżak, *op. cit.*, p. 177.

cialist North Vietnam supported Beijing's policy at that time. In the times of US army presence in Indochina, close cooperation between the two communist states was observed. This situation, however, changed significantly in the 1970s when Vietnam reoriented its policy towards Moscow. The Chinese-Vietnamese war erupted in 1979, and the mutual relations remain tense since that time.[19] On the turn of February and March 1988, the most serious military encounter in the history of the archipelagos took place between both these countries. In result, the Chinese captured few groups of islands and reefs of the Spratley archipelago. Vietnamese losses included three warships and about 80 casualties.[20]

In 1995, a dispute rose between Beijing and Manila in the issue of dependence of Mischief reef. Occurrence of PRC's navy ships in the waters surrounding the Mischief reef, located ca. 200 km from the coasts of Palawan, resulted in an immediate reaction of the Philippine authorities. In spite of the undertaken negotiations, the reef fell under Chinese control in 1999, and the situation has remained unchanged since then.[21] The capture of the Mischief reef was the last Chinese military action on such a scale in the region, yet lesser incidents, repeating from time to time, can still be observed.[22] Among the most often acts of provocation one can list: construction works or placing national symbols on objects of a transient status, dispatching fishboats to disputable areas, 'mistaken' shelling, lesser encounters, sea chases, arrests, capturing ships, as well as activity of more or less independent political groups (usually ultra-nationalists).

The game of raw materials with the use of 'soft power'

Providing the access to raw materials is one of the key, strategic objectives of Beijing. The development of Chinese economy is to a large extent dependent on crude oil and natural gas. Nowadays, about two-thirds of these raw materials are delivered to China by sea from the Middle East and Africa. The region of South China Sea also possesses significant deposits. China, however, has strong competitors here, as the demand for oil and gas in Southeast Asia grows the most rapidly. Even cautious estimations presume that if the current speed of growth of economies from

[19] Fox, *op. cit.*, p. 204.

[20] Rowiński, *op. cit.*, p. 74.

[21] Joyner, *op. cit.*, p. 54.

[22] In July 2011, a Chinese patrol prevented a Vietnamese geological expedition from executing its research, which resulted in escalation of the conflict and criticism from Hanoi. ["China and Vietnam: a timeline of conflict," *CNN*, June 28, 2011, http://www.cnn.com/2011/WORLD/asiapcf/06/27/china.vietnam.timeline/index.html (March 14, 2012).]

this region is maintained, the annual requisition will systematically grow by ca. 4.5 percent in average until 2025.[23]

Along with the growth of PRC's global importance since the time of Deng Xiaoping's reforms, the issue of the country's external image becomes more and more important as well. For a long time, China has tried to work out a certain image, denying all theses of 'Chinese threat' or territorial expansion on its side. Many declarations were made to underline the peaceful character of conducted changes and their positive aspects. In 1954, Zhou Enlai formulated the 'five rules of peaceful coexistence' which were expected to be applied in PRC's relations with foreign countries.

The Vietnamese authorities described the actions taken by PRC on the South China Sea as a "creepy expansion."[24] The policy of PRC's government, using tools characteristic for a 'soft power,' is aimed at presenting the positive image of this country on the global scene. It does not, however, equal total resignation from 'hard power.' Already in the times of Mencius, the Chinese were aware that 'soft power' is only effective when supported by 'hard' arguments. Such approach is somewhat reflected in the discussed conflict of archipelagos in this area. In parallel with high-level agreements and cooperation, a stubborn competition between the countries of the region takes place. The ambitions of the Chinese are proved by the verve of undertaken actions, mostly the huge-scale investments in some African states. In its efforts to broaden its influence, Beijing effectively uses one of its biggest advantages, i.e. huge financial means and human resources. A distressing issue, mostly from the point of view of PRC's neighbors, is the problem of growing military supremacy of this state. In 1991, the budget of the Chinese People's Liberation Army made little above RMB 30 billion, while in 2008, it already exceeded RMB 420 billion.[25] Chinese plans in a broadly considered sphere of defense are ambitious. Official declarations of November 2008 mention *inter alia* building a fleet of aircraft carriers, first of which will be commissioned already in 2015.[26] This, along with many other actions taken by the PRC's authorities, prove that their intention will be strengthening the imperial position in political, economic, military, and cultural dimension.

[23] Michael Richardson, *Energy And Geopolitics In The South China Sea*, ASEAN Studies Centre Report No. 8, Institute of Southeast Asian Studies, Singapore, 2009, p. 28.

[24] Emmers, *op. cit.*, p. 74.

[25] Thomas Coipuram, Jr., *Comparing Global Influence: China's and U.S. Diplomacy, Foreign Aid, Trade, and Investment in the Developing World CRS Report for US Congress*, Washington: Congressional Research Center, 2008, p. 66.

[26] Richardson, *op. cit.*, p. 10.

Conclusions

When trying to make any long-term forecasts of the progress of the discussed dispute, it seems necessary to ask whether the objectives of PRC's authorities include any changes in the current geopolitical order in Asia and Pacific region. The boundaries and zones of influence created after World War II restrict the Chinese field of activity to the East and South, mostly due to the strong position held there by the United States. Beijing defines its position as a partnership worth a global empire and equal treating, free from hegemony of any of the parties. One shall, however, ask if this equality can exist along with maintaining the current system, characterized by significant prevalence of the USA. The pessimistic vision of progress of the situation dominates among the researchers dealing with the dispute in the South China Sea, assuming that new tensions will occur along with the growing economic and military power of the PRC. Actions taken by the authorities of the conflicted states towards strengthening mutual cooperation are often mentioned as the key factor appeasing the tensions in this dispute. There is no doubt that economic cooperation between these states can mitigate the risk of provocations. It should be mentioned, however, that although the volume of goods exchange between the ASEAN member states and the PRC grew more than 25 times in the years 1974–1994,[27] many military encounters and lesser incidents occurred in these years, resulting in still active tensions. It seems, therefore, that economic cooperation brings significant benefits, yet does not have radical influence on the relations of the conflicted states. It does not, however, have to go this way. In the opinion of Lee Lai-to from the National University of Singapore, PRC's relations with ASEAN member states are defined mostly in the aspect of economic bonds, which can eventually lead to mitigating the disputes and tensions. On the other hand, a different opinion is expressed by Michael Richardson and Ralf Emmers, who indicate that there are many more factors negatively influencing the progress of the dispute.[28] The most often listed one is the contradiction of interests, resulting from the struggle for influence, natural resources, and territories. The nationalisms, mostly in the PRC, Vietnam, and the Philippines, are considered to be the most important barrier against improving mutual relations. The way the change in the global balance of powers progresses will depend on further modifications of the Chinese strategy, and the performance of the international surrounding.

[27] Lee Lai-to, "China's Relations with ASEAN: Partners in the 21st Century?," *Pacifica Review*, Vol. 13, No. 1, February 2001, p. 66.

[28] Emmers, *op. cit.*, p. 74.

The fact that the main seaway of global goods transport goes through the very center of the disputable area makes this conflict concerning many countries, mostly interested in unthreatened freedom of navigation in this region. In particular the USA, playing a specific role in the global system, takes care of its interest in Asia and Pacific region, but also defend their position of a global leader. Looking forward into the future one can easily claim that in the context of growing tensions and contradictions of interests avoiding any escalation of the current conflicts and occurrence of new ones will be a success.

Bibliography

Atlas geograficzny świata, ed. by Zofia Cukierka, Warszawa–Wrocław: Polskie Przedsiębiorstwo Wydawnictw Kartograficznych im. E. Romera, 1997.

Bierzanek Remigiusz, Symonides Janusz, *Prawo międzynarodowe publiczne*, Warszawa: Lexis Nexis, 2003.

"China and Vietnam: a timeline of conflict," *CNN*, June 28, 2011, http://www.cnn.com/2011/WORLD/asiapcf/06/27/china.vietnam.timeline/index.html (March 14, 2012).

Coipuram Jr. Thomas, *Comparing Global Influence: China's and U.S. Diplomacy, Foreign Aid, Trade, and Investment in the Developing World CRS Report for US Congress*, Washington: Congressional Research Center, 2008.

Emmers Ralf, *Geopolitics and Maritime Territorial Disputes in East Asia*, London: Routledge, 2010.

Haliżak Edward, *Spór o archipelagi na Morzu Południowochińskim. Historyczna debata i działania związane z przynależnością państwową Wysp Paracelskich i Spratley*, Warszawa, 2008.

Joyner Christopher C., "The Spratly Islands Dispute in the South China Sea: Problems, Policies, and Prospects for Diplomatic Accommodation," *New England Law Review*, Vol. 32, No. 3, 1998.

Lee Lai-to, "China's Relations with ASEAN: Partners in the 21st Century?," *Pacifica Review*, Vol. 13, No. 1, February 2001.

Nordhaug Kristen, *Taiwan and the South China Sea Conflict: the China Connection Revisited,* Centre for Development and the Environment, Oslo, Norway, April, 1999.

Omar Saleem, "The Spratly Islands Dispute: China Defines the New Millennium," *American University International Law Review 15*, No. 3, 2000.

Richardson Michael, *Energy And Geopolitics In The South China Sea*, ASEAN Studies Centre Report No. 8, Institute of Southeast Asian Studies, Singapore, 2009.

Rowiński Jan, *Morze Południowochińskie – region potencjalnego konfliktu w Azji*, Warszawa: PISM, 1990.

Song Yann-huei, "United States and Territorial Disputes in the South China Sea: A study of Ocean Law and Politics," *Maryland Series In Contempropary Asian Studies*, No. 1 (168), School of Law University of Maryland, 2002.

Stuart-Fox Martin, *A Short History of China and Southeast Asia: Tribute, Trade and Influence*, London: A & U Press, 2003.

Chapter Ten

Paulina Opacka

The Way to Hong Kong Handover and its Implications

The handover of Hong Kong by China is an unprecedented issue in the colonialism history. Although the colonial system in the Far East was disassembled after the World War II, the British sovereignty over Hong Kong lasted until 1997. The Hong Kong Island became a British territory in 1842 as a result of Nanjing Treaty that ended the First Opium War. The treaty obligated China to open its harbors to foreign trade ships, give some important prerogatives to the western merchants, and settle the diplomatic procedures according to the western pattern. At that time, a cession of a small rocky island was not concerned as an important matter for the Qing government. The Nanjing Treaty was followed by other humiliating agreements, called 'the unequal treaties,' that allowed the United Kingdome to extend the colony with the Kowloon Peninsula (1860), and to lease the New Territories for 99 years (1898).

For few decades, the Chinese government did not demand the reunification, because they had to focus on the internal problems and international situation. In spite of this fact, the Chinese authorities have never acknowledged the loss of Hong Kong. On the Chinese maps, the colony was always marked as an 'occupied territory,' and since 1965, the word 'colony' was no longer used also at the United Nations forum. Using the term 'refugee' for Chinese people coming to Hong Kong was solved in the same way. The Chinese claimed Hong Kong to be a part of Fujian province, so that migration was the internal matter of the country. Actually, the whole Hong Kong problem was claimed to be an internal affair of China, and according to that it was constantly refused to be discussed at the decolonization forum. There were also some economical reasons – when the country was in a huge crisis, the trade with Hong Kong was a great source of income to the Chinese budget. For instance, in 1984, over one quarter of Chinese export was addressed to Hong Kong.[1] The Chinese position remained unchanged until Mao Zedong's death in 1976. Finally, his successor, Deng Xiaoping, officially announced the reunification of Hong Kong, Macao, and Taiwan to be the priority for his government.[2]

There were three major aspects of the Hong Kong handover.[3] At first political, since there was a necessity to improve the position of the Communist Party of China after the Cultural Revolution turbulence. The second was the international prestige, since Deng used to articulate imperial aspirations of China. Obviously, any global power does not allow a colony to exist within its territory, therefore the demand regarding Hong Kong seemed to be just a matter of time. The third aspect was the Hong Kong's wealth. In year 1982, Hong Kong GDP *per capita* was fifteen times higher than in the mainland in general, and three times higher than in the three richest provinces,[4] so absorption of this market would have been really lucrative. On the other hand, Hong Kong handover was considered as a chance for peaceful Taiwan reunification. The success of reunification process might had been a strong argument for Taipei. Because of those factors, the diplomatic offensive must had been prepared and processed perfectly, and so it was.

The 99-years lease of the New Territories was coming to an end, so the decision to begin negotiations was made in the early 80s. This time, the margin was supposed to prevent any social turbulence in Hong Kong, investments' withdrawal in particular. A prompt finalization of the negotiations would have favored a smooth sovereignty transfer. The development of Special Economic Zones in the mainland would have also been beneficial for the integration of two different economical systems.[5]

Deng's government preparations took some time. At first, a new international strategy was developed, including the basic outline of reunification, and emphasizing the anti-colonialism conception. Hong Kong, Macao, and Taiwan were supposed to be retaken according to the 'one country, two systems' rules. The term was coined by Deng Xiaoping himself. International and internal politics were also subordinated to the unification plan. Simultaneously, the Chinese position in the international area was improving: diplomatic relations with the United States were established, and the People's Republic of China replaced the Republic of

[1] Andrzej Halimarski, *Chińsko-brytyjskie porozumienie w sprawie Hongkongu*, Warszawa: PISM, 1986, p. 27.

[2] *Ibid.*

[3] *Ibid.*, p. 24–30.

[4] *Ibid.*, p. 25.

[5] *Ibid.*, p. 30.

China (Taiwan) in the UNO. Under these circumstances, the diplomatic action could finally be established.

At the beginning, the plan was introduced in Washington and Tokyo, then in Europe. The Chinese were trying to convince Americans and Japanese that they would benefit from the removal of the Great Brittan from the region. Actually, they were successful, because neither the USA nor Japan supported the British aims. On 1st October 1982, *Renmin Ribao* published a note that the decision regarding the negotiation start had been made.[6] Then, Deng informed the British Prime Minister, Margaret Thatcher, about the time limit of the negotiations that was one-sidedly settled by Beijing.[7] The British government obviously criticized this move,[8] but the Chinese only stated that the agreement to negotiate with the British government was a huge concession, therefore if the agreement was not reached within two years, China would announce the policy towards Hong Kong one-sidedly.[9] That decision was motivated by the Chinese conviction, probably a right one, that the British were going to delay the talks. However, this kind of an attitude was a very significant part of the Chinese negotiating strategy – any British demands or even suggestions were being arbitrarily rejected. From the beginning, Beijing was absolutely confident about the negotiations result. Probably so did London, but the British tried to win anything for the kingdom anyway, at least an honorary solution.

Undoubtedly, most of the assets were concentrated in the hands of the Chinese. According to the international law all three treaties were signed under the threat of a use of force, and therefore were invalid. And even if they were abided, the lease of the New Territories was about to expire. It was impossible to keep only the other parts, since it would have divided the lively metropolis in half with the demarcation line running through the city center. China has never admitted the validity of the agreements, and that also worked in favor of Beijing. Beijing was also emphasizing the willingness for peaceful solution in spite of few really aggressive and strong comments that were published in early 80s by government media. Beijing also used the argument that China "did not blame the British nation for the imperial policy pursued over one hundred years ago."[10] It was completely different from the British standpoint, since Thatcher's

---

[6] *Polityka zagraniczna Chińskiej Republiki Ludowej (1982). Dokumenty i materiały*, manuscript, ed. by Jan Rowiński, Warszawa: PISM, 1987, p. 147.

[7] Halimarski, *op. cit.*, p. 45.

[8] *Polityka zagraniczna Chińskiej Republiki Ludowej (1983). Dokumenty i materiały*, manuscript, ed. by Jan Rowiński, Warszawa: PISM, 1987, p. 216.

[9] *Ibid.*, p. 217.

[10] *Polityka zagraniczna Chińskiej Republiki Ludowej (1982)...*, p. 149.

administration did not shirk responsibility. In fact, British politicians would like continue their path and keep the colony.

The general assumption of the Chinese was that they were not going to discuss *if* Hong Kong was turned back, because "Hong Kong's future is at the Chinese's discretion."[11] The only question that could be negotiated was *how* the handover was supposed to be proceeded. That completely ruined the British concept. Actually, the only thing that the British still could use as a tool of manipulation was the economy, but it was obvious that any moves in this area would be criticized by the international community. They also could not give the citizens of Hong Kong any alternative, because of the *British Nationality Act* from 1981 that changed the legal status of inhabitants of every British colony, so they could not be considered as British citizens.[12] Therefore, that could not undermine their affiliation with the Chinese nation. Also, if Beijing decided to use the army, London would not have any chance to defend the enclave.

In spite of the difficult position, the British decided to introduce a few conceptions. The first one was keeping the British administration in Hong Kong for another 20 years. The British found it reasonable to continue the democratization process, and keep the economical prosperity. That argumentation seems to be quite cynical, since the democratization was not started, and in early 80s, there were no political parties in Hong Kong. However, the prolongation of the British administration had quite a lot of followers among the colony inhabitants. Another attempt to disturb the reunification involved the Hong Kong society in the negotiations[13]. The British claimed to be morally responsible for the colony's citizens, who had to be allowed to take part in the discussion. Beijing could not agree with that because of two reasons. The first reason was that 98 percent of Hong Kong inhabitants were Chinese, therefore Great Brittan had no right to represent them. The second, unofficial reason, was that letting the society choose Hong Kong's future was risky. According to the result of the polls conducted in Hong Kong, the society would have not voted in favor of reunification, if the referendum took place. A great part of Hong Kong's citizens, from 70 to 90 percent in 1982 and 1983 were against. Although Hong Kong's population experienced mainly economical prosperity, not the Chinese centrally planned economy during the time of The Great Leap Forward or the Cultural Revolution perturbation, lots of those people were children or grandchildren of the refugees from the mainland, so the lack of credit for Beijing was quite understandable.

[11] Halimarski, *op. cit.*, p. 36.

[12] Agata Ziętek, *Międzynarodowy status Hongkongu*, Lublin: Wydawnictwo UMCS, 1997, p. 123.

[13] Halimarski, *op. cit.*, p. 41.

Almost 20 percent of young people declared, that if Hong Kong had been turned back to China, they would have left immediately.[14] Therefore, China also allowed neither public debate nor Hong Kong representatives at the negotiating table. The Chinese used all possible means, including refusing Hong Kong citizens who were supposed to represent the community to enter the country.[15]

The first round of negotiations took place in Beijing in July 1983, and another four rounds were run by October. Their content has never been revealed, and no decisions were made. After one year, when the deadline settled by Beijing was coming up to an end, Prime Minister Thatcher suggested that Hong Kong, like most of the colonies, should have become an independent state. This argument evoked a huge media storm in China, and Thatcher was accused of attempting to partition the Chinese nation.[16] The negotiating turn took place in October 1983, when London informed about preparations to transfer the Hong Kong administration after 30th June 1997.[17] From then, the negotiations finally brought some constructive effects, instead of meaningless final communiqués. Since then, only the conditions of the sovereignty transfer and keeping current economical and social system were the subjects of discussion. The next round, held in December, concerned the issues of the *Basic Law* and administrative structure.

In late 1983, Beijing set a meeting of high Chinese officials and Hong Kong elites to introduce Chinese intentions towards the future enclave status. Thanks to that move Beijing managed to gain some followers in Hong Kong, and calm the social anxiety. The conception that was introduced differed a bit from the final agreement. Deng's government assured that Hong Kong would become a Special Administrative Region with its own constitution that would be consulted with the citizens, Hong Kong harbor was supposed to remain open, and the legislation unchanged. The government in Beijing promised not to interfere with SAR's internal affairs, and not to disturb any society transformations, and the government of SAR Hong Kong was supposed to be elected without Beijing's participation.[18]

The negotiations were going ahead well, however there were still some disagreements. They regarded mainly the transitional period and Chinese participation in the administration, but also general rules of real estate, policy towards people with British Dependent Territories' passport,

---

[14] *Ibid.*

[15] *Ibid.*, p. 43.

[16] *Polityka zagraniczna Chińskiej Republiki Ludowej (1983)...*, p. 212.

[17] Ziętek, *op. cit.*, p. 116.

[18] Halimarski, *op. cit.*, p. 47.

Chinese guarantee of SAR's autonomy, and permission for the People's Liberation Army to enter the enclave.[19] The content of the negotiations was still classified, and this fact was disturbing for Hong Kong's society. Some international companies began to withdraw from the colony, and together with the announcement about the sovereignty transfer in 1997 it caused a significant stock market crash.[20] The last details were discussed on the 31st July 1984 during a direct meeting of Deng Xiaoping and Geoffrey How, the British Minister of Foreign Affairs[21]. One of the high Chinese officials commented on this event with the following words: "Charles de Gaulle is said to end the French colonialism, and now we can assume that so did the Prime Minister Margaret Thatcher with the British colonialism."[22] Two last negotiation rounds took place in September 1984. On the 19th September, the delegations completed the works on the final agreement. The document was forwarded to Beijing and London immediately, and accepted by the both sides two days later. On the 21st, the papers were signed by the heads of delegations, and finally published.[23] The official signing ceremony of the *Sino-British Joint Declaration* took place on the 19th December 1984 in Beijing. The documents were signed by the Chinese Prime Minister Zhao Ziyang and his British equivalent, Margaret Thatcher. After that, the agreement was accepted by both Queen Elizabeth II and the National People's Congress of China. The ratification instruments were exchanged in Beijing on the 27th May 1985, and from this moment, the implementation of the agreement became inevitable. For Hong Kong, that was the beginning of a 13-year-long transitional period.[24]

The *Joint Declaration* was a base document. It guaranteed an implemention of the rule 'one country, two systems,' and keeping it for another 50 years after the handover on the 30th June 1997. The document affected the whole territory of the colony, including not only the New Territories, but the Kowloon peninsula and the Hong Kong island as well. The document also mentioned the establishment of Hong Kong as a Special Administrative Region (according to the 1982 Constitution of the People's Republic of China), that was supposed to be broadly autonomous regarding the internal affairs (independent legislature, executive and judiciary), but dependent on Beijing regarding foreign and security poli-

[19] *Ibid.*, p. 49.

[20] *Trading Analysis of October 27 and 28, 1997. A Report by the Division of Market Regulation U.S. Securities and Exchange Commission*, U.S. Securities and Exchange Commission, September 1998, http://www.sec.gov/news/studies/tradrep.htm (March 15, 2012).

[21] Halimarski, *op. cit.*, p. 47.

[22] *Ibid.*

[23] *Ibid.*, p. 49.

[24] *Ibid.*, p. 50.

tics. The limitation for the autonomy was that the Chief of Executive was supposed to be nominated by the Central People's Government in Beijing on the basis of election and local consultations.

The fifth paragraph of the *Joint Declaration* guarantees that "the economical and social system of Hong Kong," and "the lifestyle" are supposed to remain unchanged. Therefore, the Hong Kong citizens are supposed to keep all rights and civil liberties, including the freedom of speech and independent media, freedom of assembly and association, religion, the right to travel abroad, strike etc. The law is to protect private property and foreign investment as well. The central government is not supposed to levy any taxes on Hong Kong. The SAR's authorities are allowed to maintain economical relations autonomously, and hold a membership of international organizations using the name 'Hong Kong-China.'

The other documents concern some particular issues of the handover. The first annex defined the Chinese policy towards the region in the next 50 years. It says that English was going to remain the official language of Hong Kong along with Chinese; Hong Kong was free to use its regional flag. There are also some details concerning the internal matters like the educational system, but also the procedures of setting up international relations, and participating in any diplomatic activities run by the central authorities if they concern Hong Kong. The second annex set up the *Sino-British Joint Liaison Group*, whose goal was "to effectively implementation the *Joint Declaration*." The Liaison Group was supposed to consult any disputes, and to prepare the sovereignty transfer procedures. Any problems that were impossible to solve at the group level were supposed to be directed to the governments of both countries. The group meetings were supposed to take place at least once a year in Beijing, Hong Kong, and London until the year 2000.[25] The other documents, two memorandums, concern the citizenship issue. The problem is the difference between the principles of the United Kingdome and China. In China, the citizenship is determined according to the right of blood (*ius sanguinis*), but in Great Britain, by the place of birth (*ius soli*). Therefore, all inhabitants of Hong Kong were recognized as Chinese, but the problem was what citizenship should be given to the non-Chinese part of this multinational society. Finally, it was decided that a special travel documents of SAR Hong Kong would be issued for them. That was kind of a privilege, because the Chinese did not obtain it. Beijing refused to give a dual citizenship to the Chinese people.

---

[25] Ziętek, *op. cit.*, p. 167–204.

The transition from a colony to a Special Administrative Region demanded new internal rules to be defined, since the previous ones were supposed to be cancelled. Therefore, immediately on signing the *Joint Declaration*, a special committee was set up. It was supposed to build up the *Basic Law* for SAR Hong Kong. The committee consisted of 59 specialists from the Mainland, and 23 from Hong Kong. The contents was approved by the Chinese Parliament on the 4th April 1990. The *Basic Law* was supposed to be a guarantee of smooth sovereignty transfer and stable development, as well as permanence of the political system. According to the *Basic Law,* it cannot be changed within the next 50 years. The 12th paragraph concerns the status of the Special Administrative Region.

Without any doubt, the agreement was a great success of Deng Xiaoping's government. The Chinese diplomacy managed to achieve everything that they meant before the negotiations started. Moreover, they did not even have to consider using military force. Besides the obvious economical profit, the prestige was the greatest achievement of China. The British officially held their diplomats in high esteem for negotiating "more basic rights and freedoms" that people could have expected.[26] In spite of that, Prime Minister Thatcher must had been aware of the actual failure. A very symbolical event was when Margaret Thatcher stumbled on her way out from the Great Hall of the People in Beijing where she was talking to Deng for over two hours. She fell down the stairs and landed on her knees right in front of a group of reporters.[27] It was September 1982, one of the crucial moments of the talks after Deng announced that the British rule in Hong Kong would expire together with the lease of the New Territories. The articles describing that incident very precise and suitably commented, with the photography of the "fallen Great Britain," were published in tens of Chinese and foreign newspapers.

That was also a full success for the Deng's new concept. Anti-colonialism and the peaceful coexistence were strongly emphasized in the international strategy of Beijing after Deng's succession. For the other countries, that was another signal that China is a serious player at the international arena, and its authorities will always do what they say. That was also significant for the credibility of Beijing's reunification plan, including Taiwan.

[26] Martin Childs, "Sir Percy Cradock: Diplomat who played a crucial role in negotiating the handover of Hong Kong to China," February 19, 2010, *The Independent*, http://www.independent.co.uk/news/obituaries/sir-percy-cradock-diplomat-who-played-a-crucial-role-in-negotiating-the-handover-of-hong-kong-to-china-1903926.html (January 29, 2012).

[27] Willy Wo-Lap Lam, "The Thatcher Treatment. China plots showdown with U.S. over Taiwan," *CNN,* November 25, 2003, http://edition.cnn.com/2003/WORLD/asiapcf/east/11/24/willy.column/index.html (March 15, 2012).

It cannot be assumed that the agreement gave the international community and Hong Kong citizens a guarantee, because it was and still is dependent of Beijing's goodwill. However, the context of Taiwan can be never omitted while considering the *Joint Declaration*. It was kind of an assurance that Beijing would put a lot of effort to succeed. From the other hand, there were some ambiguous records that could be interpreted in different ways. The 'one country, two systems' formula is very flexible, especially for the Chinese. That was a main moot point in the debate – Western politicians pointed the political separation of Hong Kong, but the Chinese emphasized that 'system' means 'economy.'[28]

The last years before the official handover were actually filled with the anxiety. The optimistic mood related to the transformation process started by Deng's government was replaced with an omnipresent fear after the Tiananmen square protests in June 1989. The violent suppression of the manifestation shocked the public opinion in Hong Kong, caused significant declines in the stock market and real estate prices. Also the number of emigrants increased from the constant quantity of twenty thousand per year in the 80s, and about thirty thousand in 1987: immediately after the Tiananmen events forty thousand people left Hong Kong, and over sixty thousand in 1992. The main directions of the migration were the United States, Canada, and Australia.[29] The Hong Kong society even tried to convince the British government to grant them British citizenship, although that was contrary to the agreements, so nothing could not be done about it. However, to protect Hong Kong from the communist regime, Margaret Thatcher's government decided to begin the democratization of the enclave. Nothing decisive could have been done, since no one wanted to provoke Beijing, but the colonial government started a huge campaign to raise the political awareness among the Hong Kong citizens. It was supposed to teach the society how to oppose the Chinese way of governance after the 1st July 1997.

As it was mentioned, the *Basic Law* says that the democratization is possible, but no specified time of the general election was given. Moreover, the result of the election may be regarded as binding only if it is accepted by the central government.[30] In 1995, a serious conflict between Hong Kong last governor, Chris Patten, and the authorities from the Mainland occurrred. From 1992, Patten was trying to push ahead a pro-

[28] Zlętek, *op. cit.*, p. 125.

[29] *Asia Pacific Migration Research Network (APMRN). Migration Issues in the Asia Pacific. Issues Paper From Hong Kong*, http://www.unesco.org/most/apmrnwp7.htm (January 29, 2012).

[30] *Ustawa Zasadnicza dla Specjalnego Regionu Administracyjnego Chińskiej Republiki Ludowej Hongkongu (Projekt)*, in: Zlętek, *op. cit.*, p. 180–205.

ject that was contrary to the agreements. In 1994, he held the elections of district councils and municipal authorities, and in 1995 – the general elections of the Legislative Council. All of those elections were a success of pro-democracy parties that have won ca. 70 percent of votes, while those related to Beijing – only about 25 percent. However, immediately after that the Beijing government announced that China would not accept the results, so all elected authorities were dissolved after the handover. That was the first attempt of Hong Kong democratization, since before 1994 the citizens did not have the right to vote, and had no actual influence on the political affairs. The electoral law was also changed from majority system to proportional. Moreover, according to the new law, less people were entitled to vote. Therefore, the democrats, in spite of the public support, did not obtain the majority in the elections to the *LegCo* in 1998.[31]

Although the Chinese promised Hong Kong a wide autonomy, the records of the *Basic Law* does not seem to be optimistic. All authorities, either elected or appointed, must be accepted by Beijing. Therefore, the first Chief Executive (equivalent of the former governor) Tung Chee-Hwa could be elected for the second term in spite of public unpopularity. To stand for the election of the Chief Executive candidates need the support of 100 members of the Election Committee,[32] and in 2002 no one else managed to get it. After his swearing-in for the second term, he launched the 'ministry system' in Hong Kong, and it was supposed to "improve management efficiency." In practice it meant that fourteen officials were nominated by the Chief Executive, with Beijing consent, to manage the new portfolios. This idea was widely criticized as another attempt to control the enclave by the people related to the central government. Some journalists found it "a proof of loyalty"[33] that Tung had to give to Beijing in exchange for his reelection. However, the circles supporting Tung still hoped that he would accelerate the democratization process, but it never happened. In 2002, the Chinese Deputy Prime Minister, Qian Qichen, stated that Hong Kong political system worked well, and there was no need to make any change.[34]

Another controversy was the problem of Article 23. That record of the *Basic Law* relates to fighting rebellion, subversion, and espionage. The

[31] *Azja Wschodnia na przełomie XX i XXI wieku. Przemiany polityczne i społeczne. Studia i szkice*, ed. Krzysztof Gawlikowski, Warszawa: Wydawnictwo TRIO, 2004, p. 151.

[32] The Election Committee consists of 800 members that represent different professions, manufacturers, businessmen, journalists, labor unions etc., and the Hong Kong representatives in the Chinese People's Political Consultative Conference. Besides, the candidate must be accepted by Beijing.

[33] Jasper Becker, *Why I Was Fired in Hong Kong*, May 4, 2002, *Washington Post*, http://www.taiwandc.org/wp-2002-08.htm (January 29, 2012).

[34] *Azja Wschodnia na przełomie XX I XXI wieku...*, *op. cit.*, p. 154.

local authorities assured that this kind of law existed in many democratic countries, and the Hong Kong society should have not be worried. However, the imprecise records were concerned a possibility for the central government to interfere in the internal affairs of the enclave. According to this law it was easy to accuse, for instance, pro-democracy organizations of subversion, or the media reporting about Taiwan of promoting secession. It could have been punished with life imprisonment.[35] The consultations were ended in 2002, and one year later, the project was supposed to be voted in the Legislative Council. That triggered mass protests.[36] Over half million people, especially the middle class, took part in the demonstrations. According to the poll launched by the Hong Kong University this protests were directed against Tung himself and the Beijing government. The great majority (from 80 to 85 percent) expressed their opposition against the new law and Tung.[37] The response of the central government was surprising. Although Beijing claimed that they were not going to withdrew the idea from the beginning, in early September 2003, all works on the law were frozen. Obviously, it is hard to judge whether this move was motivated by the protests or the international image, but that was the first time when any decisions made in Beijing were changed because of the public pressure. Officially, the suspension was just temporary, and the works were to be continued "in more favorable circumstances."[38] However, this kind of reaction was certainly a positive signal for the citizens of SAR. Another significant issue is fact that in Hong Kong, the Beijing authorities tolerate different kind of activities that are strictly forbidden in the Mainland. For instance, every year in Hong Kong a big manifestation in the memory of the Tiananmen Square protests of 1989 takes place. Another example is the Falun Gong organization.[39] It is illegal in the Mainland, but in Hong Kong, in spite of Beijing's pressure, it was not banned.

In 2005, Tung resigned from his function, officially due to health issues. According to the *Basic Law*, his office was taken over by his deputy, sir Donald Tsang. Tsang also won the election in 2007. This time there were two candidates: his opponent was Alan Leong, representative of a pro-democracy circles. It was surprising that anyone besides the Beijing candidate (Tsang) was able to gain the support of 100 members of

---

[35] *Ibid.*, p. 155.

[36] *Ibid.*

[37] Joseph Man Chan, Robert Ting-Yiu Chung, *Who can Mobilize 500,000 People to Rally? July 1 Demonstration and Political Communication in Hong Kong*, http://hkupop.hku.hk/english/columns/columns22.html (January 29, 2012).

[38] *Azja Wschodnia na przełomie XX I XXI wieku..., op. cit.*, p. 155.

[39] *Ibid.*

the Election Committee. Tsang won 649 votes to 123,[40] but according to the polls held among the citizens in the general elections Tsang's victory would not had been that obvious. During the election campaign, the candidates took part in two live transmitted TV debates. In spite of fact that the society did not have the direct influence on the election result, both of them had a large audience.[41] It is an evidence of the involvement of the Hong Kong citizens in politics. Actually, the growth of the awareness took place after the year 1997, when numerous problems started to disturb the citizens' existence, for instance the Asian financial crisis or the SARS epidemic. That issues also had an influence on the critical evaluation of Tung Chee-Hwa governance.

Although the possibility of general election is contained in the *Basic Law* it seems to be impossible to happen in the near future. In 2004, Beijing announced that the election would not be held sooner than in 2012, but in 2007, the date was moved forward again to 2017. Donald Tsang's term of office comes to an end in 2012, and one year later, the same change will take place in Beijing – President Hu Jintao and Prime Minister Wen Jiabao will end the tenure. Due to the above the future of Hong Kong is difficult to foresee.[42] However, the process of democratization is seen as enormously slow. Analytics point out the paradox of Hong Kong's relatively free and vibrant society and the lack of political transformation.[43] Ma Ngok, professor of Chinese University of Hong Kong, defines it as "a special case, as it has a highly developed civil society without culmination in a democratic political regime."[44] There is no agreement as for the reasons of this discrepancy are concerned. Some commentators put the blame on the Hong Kong society, but we cannot forget SAR's situation. Beijing's willingness to make concessions under the public pressure has got its limitations, and probably for now that is the possible maximum.

The success of Hong Kong handover is actually indisputable. The first years showed that the life style did not really change. Hong Kong defended also its economical position, and improved in new areas, for instance by launching several impressive tourist projects. In spite of the difficul-

---

[40] *The Third Term Chief Executive Election. Election Results*, March 25, 2007, http://www.elections.gov.hk/ce2007/eng/result.html (January 29, 2012).

[41] Michael F. Martin, *Hong Kong: Ten Years After Handover*, Congressional Research Service, June 29, 2007, http://www.fas.org/sgp/crs/row/RL34071.pdf (January 29, 2012).

[42] Donald Greenlees, *China Will Make Hong Kong Wait to Elect Leader,* December 30, 2007, http://www.nytimes.com/2007/12/30/world/asia/30hong.html?_r=1&oref=slogin (January 29, 2012).

[43] Ma Ngok, "Civil Society and Democratization in Hong Kong Paradox and Duality," *Taiwan Journal of Democracy*, Vol. 4, No. 2, December 2008, p. 156, http://www.tfd.org.tw/docs/dj0402/155-176%20MA%20Ngok.pdf (January 29, 2012).

[44] *Ibid.*, p. 158.

ties of the Asian crisis and SARS epidemic, the economy kept growing. However, the fact that the purpose was to test the 'one country,two systems' formula, and then use it as a strong argument for Taipei is worth emphasizing. The transition is still under careful international observation. Naturally, one of the major observers is Taipei, and its opinion is not really positive. It is easily noticeable while reading the reports that are published every year by the Taiwanese Mainland Affairs Office. All the reports very precisely, and with examples, point out the Chinese violation of the promises made before the implementation of the Deng's formula in Hong Kong. Using the publicly available information, the MAC has found 178 controversial cases. The main accusations are the Beijing's control over the members of the Hong Kong's authorities, Chinese interference in the internal affairs of the enclave (judicial power, economics etc.), restrain of civil liberties and the freedom of speech.[45] The Taiwanese also will remember the political manipulation in the Hong Kong-Taiwan relations, when Beijing pressured the authorities of Hong Kong to restrain the official contacts between them to minimum. That was the situation in Hong Kong until the pro-Beijing party seized power in Taipei in 2008.[46] Therefore, it seems reasonable to say that Beijing needs to find another way for Taiwan. The differences between Hong Kong and the Republic of China are significant, and the territories cannot be treated in the same way. If Beijing still wants to use the 'one country, two systems' formula, it must certainly be vastly modified for Taiwan. And that is the new challenge for the reunited China.

Bibliography

Asia Pacific Migration Research Network (APMRN). Migration Issues in the Asia Pacific. Issues Paper From Hong Kong, http://www.unesco.org/most/apmrnwp7.htm (January 29, 2012).

Azja Wschodnia na przełomie XX i XXI wieku. Przemiany polityczne i społeczne. Studia i szkice, ed. by Krzysztof Gawlikowski, Warszawa: Wydawnictwo TRIO, 2004.

Becker Jasper, *Why I Was Fired in Hong Kong*, May 4, 2002, *Washington Post*, http://www.taiwandc.org/wp-2002-08.htm (January 29, 2012).

[45] All analysis reports published by MAC available on-line: http://www.mac.gov.tw/lp.asp?ctNode=5939&CtUnit=4157&BaseDSD=7&mp=3 (January 29, 2012).

[46] Jun-han Chu, *Taiwan and Hong Kong Re-embrace Each Other*, January 2010, http://www.hkjournal.org/PDF/2010_spring/3.pdf (January 29, 2012).

Chan Joseph Man, Chung Robert Ting-Yiu, *Who Can Mobilize 500,000 People to Rally? July 1 Demonstration and Political Communication in Hong Kong*, http://hkupop.hku.hk/english/columns/columns22.html (January 29, 2012).

Childs Martin, "Sir Percy Cradock: Diplomat who played a crucial role in negotiating the handover of Hong Kong to China," February 19, 2010, *The Independent*, http://www.independent.co.uk/news/obituaries/sir-percy-cradock-diplomat-who-played-a-crucial-role-in-negotiating-the-handover-of-hong-kong-to-china-1903926.html (January 29, 2012).

Chu Jun-han, *Taiwan and Hong Kong Re-embrace Each Other*, January 2010, http://www.hkjournal.org/PDF/2010_spring/3.pdf (January 29, 2012).

Greenlees Donald, *China Will Make Hong Kong Wait to Elect Leader*, December 30, 2007, http://www.nytimes.com/2007/12/30/world/asia/30hong.html?_r=1&oref=slogin (January 29, 2012).

Halimarski Andrzej, *Chińsko-brytyjskie porozumienie w sprawie Hongkongu*, Warszawa: PISM, 1986.

Lam Willy Wo-Lap, "The Thatcher Treatment. China plots showdown with U.S. over Taiwan," *CNN*, November 25, 2003, http://edition.cnn.com/2003/WORLD/asiapcf/east/11/24/willy.column/index.html (March 15, 2012).

Ma Ngok, "Civil Society and Democratization in Hong Kong Paradox and Duality", *Taiwan Journal of Democracy*, Vol. 4, No. 2, December 2008, http://www.tfd.org.tw/docs/dj0402/155-176%20MA%20Ngok.pdf (January 29, 2012).

Martin Michael F., *Hong Kong: Ten Years After Handover*, Congressional Research Service, June 29, 2007, http://www.fas.org/sgp/crs/row/RL34071.pdf (January 29, 2012).

Polityka zagraniczna Chińskiej Republiki Ludowej (1982). Dokumenty i materiały, manuscript, ed. by Jan Rowiński, Warszawa: PISM, 1987.

Polityka zagraniczna Chińskiej Republiki Ludowej (1983). Dokumenty i materiały, manuscript, ed. by Jan Rowiński, Warszawa: PISM, 1987.

The Third Term Chief Executive Election. Election Results, March 25, 2007, http://www.elections.gov.hk/ce2007/eng/result.html (January 29, 2012).

Trading Analysis of October 27 and 28, 1997. A Report by the Division of Market Regulation U.S. Securities and Exchange Commission, U.S. Securities and Exchange Commission, September 1998, http://www.sec.gov/news/studies/tradrep.htm (March 15, 2012).

Ustawa Zasadnicza dla Specjalnego Regionu Administracyjnego Chińskiej Republiki Ludowej Hongkongu (Projekt), in: Agata Ziętek, *Międzynarodowy status Hongkongu*, Lublin: Wydawnictwo UMCS, 1997.

Ziętek Agata, *Międzynarodowy status Hongkongu*, Lublin: Wydawnictwo UMCS, 1997.

Technical editor
Anna Poinc-Chrabąszcz

Proofreader
Gabriela Niemiec

Typesetter
Katarzyna Mróz-Jaskuła

Jagiellonian University Press
Office: ul. Michałowskiego 9/2, 31-126 Kraków
Phone: 12-631-18-81, 12-631-18-82, Fax: 12-631-18-83